this little dish®

family cookbook

belongs to the

family

For Monty & Ridley

SPHERE

First published in Great Britain in 2015 by Sphere

Copyright © Healthy Kids Ltd 2015

Photos © Haarala Hamilton Photography
Design by Sian Rance and Emil Dacanay at D.R.ink
Little Dish illustrations by Claudio Vecchio
Illustrations on p.12–13 and p.186-187 by Sian Rance

A CIP catalogue record for this book
is available from the British Library.

ISBN 978-0-7515-5975-0

Printed and bound in China

Sphere
An imprint of
Little, Brown Book Group
Carmelite House
50 Victoria Embankment
London EC4Y 0DZ

An Hachette UK Company
www.hachette.co.uk

www.littlebrown.co.uk

the little dish® family cookbook

Hillary Graves

Contents

Introduction

Establishing healthy eating habits at an early age is crucial, but home cooking every night of the week can be challenging for busy families. At Little Dish we make delicious, healthy food that kids love to eat and mums feel great about serving because we only use 100 per cent natural ingredients.

At Little Dish we share a passion for making a positive difference in children's nutrition and creating the best tasting children's food with the highest nutritional standards.

Everyone at Little Dish loves to cook. A few years ago we published *The Little Dish Favourites Cookbook*, a collection of our favourite recipes for weaning your baby; preparing simple family meals; and creating healthy treats and puddings. Throughout the book we indicated which steps were perfect for little hands to get children involved, and the response was so positive that we decided to dedicate our next cookbook entirely to kids and cooking.

My children, Monty and Ridley (aged eight and six as I write), have always been drawn to whatever I am doing in the kitchen. Even before they were walking, they loved playing with pots, pans and a wooden spoon. As they got older they started asking for things from the cupboard to put in their pots, such as dried pasta, filling one pan then another, mixing along the way.

Children who learn how to cook before the age of eight are 50 per cent more likely to have a healthy diet later in life. It is a fundamental life skill that can not only influence good health but also encourage fun and creativity.

My elder son Monty and I started cooking together when he was 18 months old, using simple recipes like Fruit muffins (p.28) and Grandma's lemon cake (p.178). I was amazed that even at such a young age he had so much fun pouring in the ingredients, mixing everything up and waiting impatiently for the result to emerge from the oven. The very best part, of course, was the tasting. We have expanded our repertoire over the years, and the boys now like making all kinds of recipes, not just treats. Better still, when they are involved in the preparation of the dish, they are more inclined to want to eat it.

Cooking with your children is not only a lovely way to spend time together, but a way of providing them with an invaluable lifelong skill. There is momentum building in the UK around kids and cooking, including the new School Food Plan and the fact that cooking is part of the National Curriculum again. Children who learn how to cook before the age of eight are 50 per cent more likely to have a healthy diet later in life. It is a fundamental life skill that can not only influence good health but also encourage fun and creativity.

In each of the recipes that follow, there is a role for children which we indicate in the speech bubble on the bottom left corner so as you progress through the book, children

Like everything we make at Little Dish, which is approved by our panel of tiny tasters and their parents, every recipe we've included here has been tested with great success and loved by both children and adults.

know exactly where to look for their special instructions. And as they develop their skills (from adding and stirring ingredients, to grating cheese, to forming meatballs, to cracking an egg, and beyond) they can track their progress on their 'little chef's skills chart' on p.10 by adding stickers as they complete various tasks. You'll find an assortment of stickers for them to choose from included in the book.

We've also created some fun, educational sections such as learning about kitchen equipment on p.12–13 and the importance of eating a rainbow of fruits and vegetables on p.188–199.

While the focus of this book is getting your kids involved, the recipes we have developed and chosen are tried and trusted favourites which can be enjoyed by the whole family. Like everything we make at Little Dish, which is approved by our panel of tiny tasters and their parents, every recipe we've included here has been tested with great success and loved by both children and adults.

These recipes have become staples in our homes. We hope they are equally as useful to you and bring the same excitement and delight to your children as they do to ours.

Hillary Graves, 2015

A note on ingredients

The ingredients we use in this book are appropriate for children from the age of one year if they don't have any allergies.

- *Children under one should not drink cow's milk (only breast milk or formula). However small quantities of full-fat cow's milk can be used in cooking from the age of seven months.*

- *Children under one should not have honey.*

- *Speak to your GP before introducing nuts to children under one.*

The little chef's skills chart

We've grouped our cooking skills into 3 stages to help you chart your little chef's progress, but of course you'll know best when they're ready to try something a bit trickier. Each time they try a new skill, help them pop a sticker on to show what they've achieved. Before you know it, they'll work their way towards earning their little chef's apron.

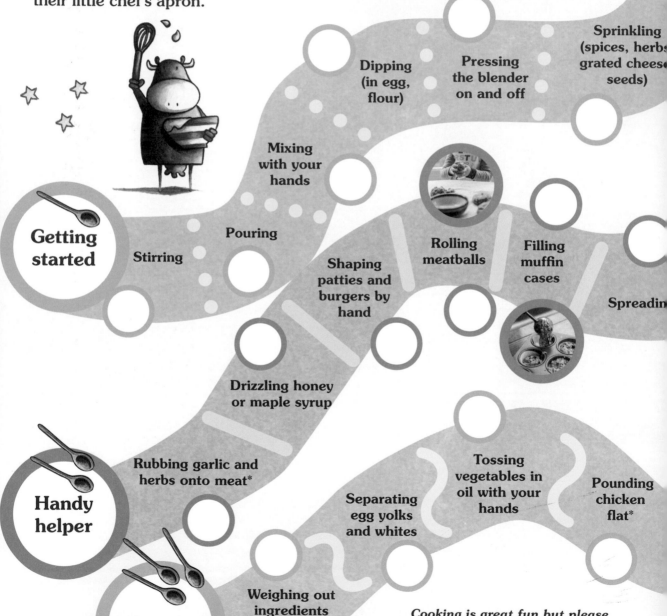

Dipping (in egg, flour)

Pressing the blender on and off

Sprinkling (spices, herbs, grated cheese, seeds)

Mixing with your hands

Getting started

Pouring

Stirring

Rolling meatballs

Filling muffin cases

Shaping patties and burgers by hand

Spreading

Drizzling honey or maple syrup

Rubbing garlic and herbs onto meat*

Tossing vegetables in oil with your hands

Pounding chicken flat*

Handy helper

Separating egg yolks and whites

Weighing out ingredients

Little chef

Cooking is great fun but please make sure you're keeping a close eye on safety at all times.

Squeezing lemon

Crumbling or grating cheese

Finished **'getting started'?** Email us a photo of your little one with their chart completed to this stage and we'll send them a certificate

Topping pizzas

Brushing pastry (with egg, butter)

Breaking broccoli or cauliflower into florets

Picking herb leaves off stalks

to
....
for getting started

little **dish**

Bashing (cornflakes, meringues)

Mashing (banana, potato)

Layering ingredients

Grating carrot or courgette

Rubbing butter in flour (pastry, crumble)

Cracking eggs

Is your little one a **'handy helper'** now? Email us a photo of them demonstrating one of their new skills and we'll send them a medal

Whisking (electric)

Making foil parcels (fish in foil)

Remember always to wash little hands well after touching raw meat

Whisking (manual)

Putting fruit on skewers

Congrats – now you have a **little chef** in your kitchen! Send us a photo of them with their completed chart and we'll send them a Little Dish little chef's apron

little **dish**

Getting to know your pots and pans

Every cook has cupboards, shelves and drawers full of all kinds of interesting cooking utensils. See which ones your little helper can name already, and use this page to help them find things you need for today's recipe.

Kettle

Toaster

Pastry brush

Colander

Rolling pin

Frying pans

Saucepans

Roasting trays

Electric whisk   Oven glove   Whisk   Spatula   Tongs   Ladle   Apron   Ice cream scoop

Potato masher   Wooden spoon   Blender   Food processor   Measuring spoons

Chopping board   Grater   Pepper grinder

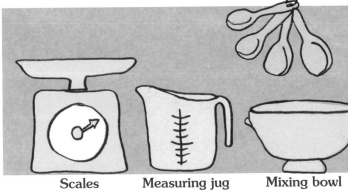

Scales   Measuring jug   Mixing bowl

Storage pots   Lemon juicer

Muffin tray

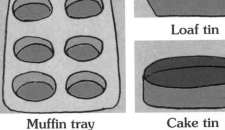

Loaf tin

Cake tin   Cookie cutters

Breakfast

It's been said that breakfast is the most important meal of the day. Especially for growing children who have (hopefully) had a good, long sleep and are ready to be refuelled for the day ahead.

Unfortunately many breakfast foods you buy in the supermarket, including most packaged cereals, are high in sugar and low in important nutrients. The breakfast recipes we've put together here are easy to make with a focus on fruit, grains and protein, and all have a role for your children to help prepare.

Breakfast can also be a nice time to sit together as a family before everyone heads off on their busy day.

Bircher muesli

This is an easy no-cook breakfast which your children can help you assemble the night before. It sets in the fridge overnight and is ready when you wake up.

Makes

approximately 4 servings

Prep time

20–25 minutes

Ingredients

100g rolled oats

100g plain, natural yoghurt

100ml full-fat or semi-skim milk (or substitute almond milk (p.43) or cashew milk (p.43))

75g mixed berries, lightly crushed

2 tablespoons honey

50g mixed seeds (optional)

Method

In a medium bowl, mix together the oats, yoghurt, milk, berries and honey. Divide amongst 4 little jam jars or ramekins and sprinkle over the seeds if using. Place in the fridge to chill overnight.

I can help weigh out the ingredients and stir the mixture

Fruit porridge

A warm bowl of porridge is a great way to start the day. Try one of the fresh nut milks on p.43 for a dairy-free alternative. Kids love to help stir in the fruit and drizzle the honey.

Serves

a family of 4

Prep time

5 minutes

Cook time

5 minutes

Ingredients

200g rolled oats

450ml full-fat or semi-skim milk (or substitute almond milk (p.43) or cashew milk (p.43))

1 tablespoon ground flaxseed

1 apple, roughly chopped; 200g blackberries and/or 1 banana, mashed

Drizzle of honey, to serve (optional)

Method

Put the oats and milk into a medium pan over a medium heat. Bring to a simmer for 5–6 minutes stirring occasionally until the porridge is cooked and creamy. Stir in the flaxseed and the apple, berries or banana. Serve with a drizzle of honey if using.

Cinnamon French toast

Makes
4 pieces

Prep time
5 minutes

Cook time
4–6 minutes

Ingredients

2 medium free-range eggs

1 tablespoon milk

Pinch of ground cinnamon

Knob of butter

4 slices of bread (wholemeal, sourdough or fruit and nut bread all work well)

Apple compote (p.22) or maple syrup, to serve

Method

1. Crack the eggs into a large bowl. Stir in the milk and beat with a fork. Add the cinnamon.

2. Place the butter in a large frying pan over a low heat.

3. Dip a slice of the bread into the egg mixture. Turn over the bread and dip again to make sure it's well covered with the egg mixture. Let the excess egg drip off the bread and then put straight into the frying pan. Repeat with the remaining slices of bread, adding more butter to the pan if needed.

4. Increase the heat to medium and cook each slice for 2 minutes on each side or until golden. Carefully remove from the pan and serve with Apple compote or maple syrup.

I can help whisk together the eggs and milk and dip the bread into the eggy mixture

Apple compote

This is a topping for Cinnamon French toast (p.21) or Pancakes (p.31). Also very popular on its own for breakfast, as an after-school snack or a healthy pudding. It can be served hot or cold.

Serves
2 or as a topping
for 4 slices of
French toast

Prep time
10 minutes

Cook time
10–15 minutes

Ingredients

225g eating apples (approximately 2 medium apples), chopped (skin left on)

Squeeze of lemon juice

2 tablespoons water

1 teaspoon brown sugar (optional)

Method

1. Place the chopped apples in a small saucepan with the lemon juice and 2 tablespoons water. Cover with a lid and simmer over a low heat for 10–15 minutes or until very soft, stirring occasionally.

2. Remove from the heat and add the brown sugar to sweeten if needed. Stir until well combined.

I can help squeeze the lemon juice on the apples and sprinkle in the brown sugar

Boiled eggs and soldiers

Children can help make the 'soldiers' by using a pair of kids' safety scissors to cut the toast or pitta into strips.

Serves
2

Prep time
5 minutes

Cook time
4–5 minutes

Ingredients

2 medium free-range eggs

2 slices of wholegrain bread or brown pitta

Method

1. Fill a small pan with water and place on the hob. Gently bring to the boil. When the water starts to boil, gently lower the eggs into the water and boil for 5 minutes (4 minutes if the eggs have been stored at room temperature).

2. Meanwhile, place the bread or pitta in the toaster.

3. Remove the eggs with a large slotted spoon and plunge them in a bowl of cold water. This will stop the eggs cooking. Place in egg cups and cut the tops off the eggs.

4. Cut the toast or pitta bread into soldiers so kids can dip into the runny egg.

I can help cut the soldiers for dipping

Low-sugar granola

This granola is super easy to make and can be stored in the cupboard in an airtight container for 2–3 weeks. It tastes great with and without the nuts, depending on what your children prefer. Serve with milk, nut milk (p.43), yoghurt (p.27) or on its own as a little snack.

Makes
8–10 servings

Prep time
10 minutes

Cook time
45 minutes

Ingredients

240g rolled oats

50g desiccated coconut

100g mixed nuts, coarsely chopped

2 tablespoons olive oil

6 tablespoons maple syrup

1 teaspoon ground cinnamon

1 medium free-range egg white

100g mixed dried fruit such as cranberries or chopped apricots (optional)

Method

1. Preheat the oven to 150°C/gas mark 2. Line a large baking tray with baking parchment.

2. In a large bowl, combine the oats, coconut, nuts, oil, maple syrup and cinnamon. In a separate small bowl, whisk the egg white until frothy and stir it into the granola mixture.

3. Spread the granola mixture onto the prepared tray. Bake for 45 minutes, turning once during cooking. Set aside and allow to cool completely.

4. Break up the cold granola and stir in the dried fruit, if using. Store in an airtight container for 2–3 weeks.

I can help mix the ingredients, whisk the egg white and use my hands to spread the granola mixture across the baking tray

Fruit yoghurt pots

These pots will work well with any yoghurt and fruit combination you and your family choose. Divide up pots amongst your children for layering.

Makes
6 pots

Prep time
15 minutes

Ingredients

180g Low-sugar granola (p.24)

180g vanilla or Greek yoghurt

180g mixed fresh fruit (berries, mango, chopped banana etc.)

Method

Divide the granola equally between 6 small pots or ramekins. Spoon the yoghurt equally between the pots and top with the fruit. Serve immediately.

I can help layer the ingredients in the pots

Healthy fruit muffins

These muffins are best eaten on the same day they are made, especially when they are warm from the oven. Children can help add fruit to the batter, stir the ingredients, and scoop into the muffin tin. Leftovers freeze well and can be defrosted for an after-school snack.

Makes
12 muffins

Prep time
15 minutes

Cook time
20 minutes

Ingredients

Butter or cooking spray for greasing

125g white spelt flour

60g wholewheat spelt flour

60g rolled oats

40g brown sugar

3 teaspoons baking powder

2 tablespoons ground flaxseed

1 eating apple, chopped
(skin left on)

200g fresh berries, blueberries, blackberries and raspberries all work well

2 medium free-range eggs

175ml full-fat or semi-skim milk

40g butter, melted

1 teaspoon vanilla extract

Method

1. Preheat the oven to 190°C/gas mark 5. Grease a 12-hole muffin tin.

2. Mix the dry ingredients together in a bowl, then stir in the fruit.

3. Beat the eggs in a separate bowl and then stir in the milk, melted butter and vanilla extract.

4. Pour the wet ingredients into the dry ingredients and fold together, being careful not to over-mix. Using an ice cream scoop, evenly distribute the mixture into the greased tin. Bake for 20 minutes or until cooked in the middle and a skewer inserted into the centre of a muffin comes out clean.

5. Remove from the oven and allow to cool for 10 minutes then transfer to a wire rack.

Tip: To freeze, transfer the cooled muffins to an airtight container and freeze for up to 1 month.

I can help mix the ingredients and use an ice cream scoop to spoon the batter into the greased tin

Pancakes

This is an easy pancake recipe which can be made in advance and kept in the fridge for a couple of days so you can whip up pancakes even on mornings when you are short on time. I use spelt flour which has more nutrients than plain flour but you can use any flour you have on hand (in this recipe and the ones that follow).

Makes
approximately 24
9cm pancakes

Prep time
10 minutes plus
30 minutes
standing time

Cook time
2–3 minutes per
pancake

Ingredients

1 tablespoon baking powder

Pinch of salt (optional)

2 medium free-range eggs

30g butter, melted

300ml full-fat or semi-skim milk

225g spelt flour

Spray oil or butter, for cooking

Method

1. Put all the ingredients in a bowl and whisk together. Pour into a jug and leave to stand for 30 minutes in the fridge.

2. Spray a 30cm frying pan with oil and place over a medium heat. When hot add about 2 tablespoons of batter to the pan. Cook for about 1 minute on each side, when the top of the pancake starts to bubble, turn it over with a palette knife.

3. Keep warm in a low oven until ready to serve.

I can help crack the eggs into the bowl and whisk the ingredients together

Breakfast bars

Low in sugar and great on the go for breakfast or a snack. While preparing the ingredients, delegate the banana peeling and mashing to your little helpers.

Makes

8 5 x 10cm bars

Prep time

10 minutes

Cook time

25 minutes

You will need
a 20cm square
baking tin

I can help peel and mash the banana and press down the mixture in the baking tin

Ingredients

Butter or cooking spray for greasing

150g dried cranberries

75g mixed seeds

150g rolled oats

3 tablespoons coconut or olive oil

25g butter

75g honey

1 ripe banana, mashed

Method

1. Preheat the oven to 180°C/gas mark 4. Grease and line a 20cm square tin with baking parchment.

2. Put the dry ingredients into a large bowl and mix well.

3. Put the oil, butter and honey into a medium pan and stir with a wooden spoon until melted. Cook for 2 minutes. Remove from the heat and pour over the dry ingredients in the bowl. Stir in the mashed banana and mix well.

4. Pour the mixture into the baking tin and press the mixture down with a spatula, to form an even layer. Bake for 25 minutes. Leave to cool completely, and then cut into 5 x 10cm bars.

Tip: You can store these in an airtight container for a few days or in the fridge for up to a week.

Banana nut butter toast

This is a great combination of flavours and a real energy boost for the day. It's not difficult to make your own nut butter (see Homemade almond butter, below) or you can always substitute store-bought almond or cashew butter or even organic peanut butter. Just be sure to look for the brands that don't add any sugar.

Makes
1 piece

Prep time
5 minutes

Ingredients

1 piece of toast (sourdough or fruit bread work well)

Homemade almond butter or store-bought

1 banana, chopped

A small drizzle of honey (optional)

Method

Spread the toast with a thin layer of nut butter and top with chopped banana. Drizzle the honey if using.

Homemade almond butter

Makes
1 jar

Prep time
30 minutes

Ingredients

320g almonds

Pinch of salt (optional)

Method

1. Pre-heat oven to 200°C/gas mark 6.

2. Spread the almonds in a single layer in a baking dish and roast for 12–15 minutes, watching carefully not to burn. Toss half way through. When the almonds look golden, remove from oven and let cool.

3. Add nuts and salt to food processor and whiz until smooth and creamy – about 15 minutes, or until you get the texture you want.

4. Store in fridge in airtight container for up to 2 weeks.

Scrambled eggs

This was the first dish my son Monty could make on his own. He started by helping to whisk the eggs and then as he got older he would stand on a stool next to me giving the eggs a stir in the pan. It was a good way to teach him how important it is to be safe and sensible around a hot stove and oven. It's an easy recipe for children to build up to doing all on their own.

Serves
a family of 4

Prep time
5 minutes

Cook time
4–5 minutes

Ingredients

8 medium free-range eggs

Splash of milk

Knob of butter

Salt and freshly ground black pepper (optional)

Method

1. Break the eggs into a large jug and whisk in the milk with a fork.

2. Melt the butter in a frying pan and swirl it around to coat the base of the pan.

3. Pour in the eggs and stir slowly with a spatula over a low heat. Remove from the heat when the eggs are just cooked. Season to taste and serve immediately.

Variation: Add 1 teaspoon of finely chopped fresh herbs or 1 tablespoon of grated Cheddar cheese to the egg mixture before cooking.

I can help whisk together the eggs and milk

Homemade sausage patties

Children love sausages but some of the shop-bought varieties contain unhealthy ingredients such as nitrates or other preservatives. By making your own, you know exactly what's in them. Children can help mix the ingredients together and shape into patties.

Makes
8 small patties

Prep time
10 minutes plus
45 minutes
chilling

Cook time
6–8 minutes

Ingredients

500g ground pork

2 garlic cloves, finely chopped

1 tablespoon dried sage

½ tablespoon dried thyme

Pinch of ground nutmeg

½ teaspoon salt (optional)

½ teaspoon black pepper

1 medium free-range egg

Butter or cooking spray for frying

Method

1. Line a baking sheet with foil or parchment paper.
2. In a large bowl, mix together the pork, garlic, sage, thyme, nutmeg, salt and pepper. Mix well and then stir in the egg until well combined.
3. Cover the bowl with cling film and chill the mixture in the fridge for 30 minutes.
4. Shape the meat mixture into 8 equal-sized patties and place on the prepared baking sheet. Chill the patties for 15 minutes.
5. Heat the oil in a large, non-stick frying pan over a medium heat. Fry the patties for 3–4 minutes on each side, until cooked through and golden brown.

Tip: Chilled patties can be frozen. Defrost thoroughly before cooking as above.

I can help to combine the mixture with my hands and shape into patties. I always remember to wash my hands well after touching raw meat

Oven omelette

This is an easy way to make eggs for a group. You just mix all the ingredients together and bake in the oven. The egg mixture can be made up to 24 hours ahead and kept in the fridge overnight; remove 20 minutes before cooking and then follow the baking instructions below.

Serves
4–6

Prep time
5–10 minutes

Cook time
25 minutes

Ingredients

8 free-range eggs

125ml full fat milk

100g grated Cheddar cheese

50g onion, finely chopped

30g fresh spinach, finely chopped

Salt and freshly ground pepper (optional)

Method

1. Preheat the oven to 190°C/gas mark 5.

2. Lightly grease a 23cm x 16cm baking dish.

3. Beat the eggs in a large bowl and whisk in the milk. Stir in the cheese, onion and spinach. Season with salt and pepper and pour into the greased dish.

4. Bake for 25 minutes, or until the top is golden and the middle is cooked through. Cover with foil if the top starts to get too brown before the middle is cooked through.

5. Let cool for 5 minutes and serve.

I can help grate the cheese, whisk the eggs and mix the ingredients together

Pumpkin bread

This bread is great on its own warm from the oven or toasted the next day and topped with jam or nut butter (p.35). The full tin of pumpkin purée makes two loaves, so you can keep one in the freezer for another time. Just take out the night before and defrost overnight. (Or halve the recipe to make one loaf.)

Makes
2 loaves

Prep time
15 minutes

Cook time
45 minutes

Ingredients

Butter or cooking spray for greasing

210g white spelt flour

210g wholemeal spelt flour

2 teaspoons bicarbonate of soda

2 teaspoons mixed spice

1 teaspoon ground ginger

½ teaspoon cinnamon

60g brown sugar

4 medium free-range eggs, lightly beaten

425g can pumpkin purée

6 tablespoons honey

120ml olive oil

120g Greek yoghurt

I can help measure out the spices and mix the ingredients

Method

1. Preheat the oven to 180°C/gas mark 4. Grease 2 x 450g loaf tins.
2. In a large bowl, mix together all the dry ingredients. In a separate bowl whisk together the eggs, pumpkin purée, honey, olive oil and yoghurt.
3. Pour the wet ingredients into the dry ingredients and fold together, being careful not to over-mix.
4. Pour the batter into the prepared tins and bake in the oven for 45 minutes or until a skewer inserted into the centre of the loaf comes out clean.
5. Remove from the oven and allow to cool in the tin for 5 minutes. Turn onto a wire rack and allow to cool before serving.

Fresh nut milks

Nut milk is surprisingly easy to make with a good blender. All you need are some pre-soaked nuts, water and a pinch of salt. These are good on their own or as an ingredient in porridge, muesli and smoothies. For the almond milk recipe we recommend using a cheese cloth to drain the milk (available online), as it really makes a difference in terms of smoothness. However the cashew milk doesn't require this extra step.

Almond milk

 Makes 500ml

 Prep time 5 minutes plus soaking overnight

Ingredients

75g whole blanched almonds, soaked in cold water in the fridge overnight

500ml water

Pinch of salt

½ teaspoon vanilla extract (optional)

1 fresh date (optional)

Pinch of ground cinnamon (optional)

Method

1. Drain the almonds and discard the soaking water.

2. Place the almonds, water and salt in a blender and whiz until well combined. Add the vanilla, dates and cinnamon (if using) and whiz again.

3. Place the cheesecloth over a large jug and pour the milk over. Pour the strained milk into a sealable bottle and store in the fridge for up to 4 days.

Cashew milk

 Makes 500ml

 Prep time 5 minutes plus soaking overnight

Ingredients

75g cashews, soaked in cold water in the fridge overnight

500ml water

Pinch of salt

½ teaspoon vanilla extract (optional)

1 teaspoon finely chopped dried dates or ½ fresh date (optional)

Pinch of ground cinnamon (optional)

Method

1. Drain the cashews and discard the soaking water.

2. Place the cashews, water and salt in a blender and whiz until well combined. Add the vanilla, dates and cinnamon (if using) and whiz again.

3. Pour the milk into a sealable bottle and store in the fridge for up to 4 days.

Tip: Nut milks can also replace regular milk in most baking recipes.

Smoothies

Smoothies are a great way to get fruit, vegetables and nutrients into your children in a delicious way. Serve them at breakfast or as a healthy snack or pudding.

The recipes that follow are easily amended depending on what ingredients you have. Kids love to get involved – measuring out fruit, peeling bananas, throwing everything into the blender and flipping the switch to watch everything whiz together.

I find coconut water to be an excellent ingredient for smoothies as it is low in sugar and full of potassium, however, if you prefer simply substitute filtered water. Another great (optional) ingredient is ground flaxseed which is high in fibre and Omega-3.

I can help prepare the fruit and add ingredients to the blender

Sunshine orange smoothie

 Serves 4

Prep time 5 minutes

Method

Add the coconut water then the rest of the ingredients to a blender and whiz on high for at least 1 minute or until smooth. Pour into cups and serve.

Ingredients

400ml coconut water or cold water

100ml orange juice or juice of 1 orange

200g mango, diced

150g carrots, sliced into 1cm pieces

1 tablespoon ground flaxseed (optional)

Handful of ice cubes

Purple smoothie

 Serves 4

Prep time 5 minutes

Method

Place all the ingredients in a blender and whiz on high for at least 1 minute or until smooth. Pour into cups and serve.

Ingredients

400ml coconut water or cold water

1 banana, thickly sliced

1 ripe avocado, sliced

300g blueberries

1 tablespoon ground flaxseed (optional)

Handful of ice cubes

Green smoothie

 Serves 4

Prep time 5 minutes

Method

Put all the ingredients into a blender and whiz on high for at least 1½ minutes or until smooth. Blend the spinach in batches if it doesn't fit in the blender all at once. Pour into cups and serve.

Ingredients

250ml coconut water or cold water

200g spinach

150ml apple juice

1 banana, thickly sliced

½ avocado, sliced

1 tablespoon ground flaxseed (optional)

Handful of ice cubes

Red smoothie

 Serves 4

 Prep time 10 minutes

Method

Put all the ingredients in a blender, pulse for a few seconds and then whiz on high for at least 1 minute until smooth. Pour into cups and serve.

Ingredients

400ml coconut water

75ml apple juice

150g raspberries

200g strawberries, hulled and halved

1 tablespoon ground flaxseed (optional)

Handful of ice cubes

Vanilla shake

 Serves 4

 Prep time 5 minutes

Method

Put all the ingredients into a blender and whiz on high for 1 minute or until smooth. Pour into cups and serve.

Ingredients

400ml almond (p.43) or cashew (p.43) milk (or substitute full-fat or semi-skim milk)

2 teaspoons vanilla extract

1 banana, sliced

2 tablespoons honey or maple syrup

Handful of ice cubes

Chocolate shake

 Serves 4

 Prep time 5 minutes

Method

Put all the ingredients into a blender and whiz on high for 1 minute or until smooth. Pour into cups and serve.

Ingredients

400ml almond (p.43) or cashew (p.43) milk (or substitute full-fat or semi-skim milk)

2 tablespoons maple syrup

1 banana, sliced

2 tablespoons cocoa powder or raw cacao

Handful of ice cubes

Lunch and supper

There are a lot of 'children's cookbooks' on the market which are focused on making the sweet stuff, like biscuits and cakes. While making puddings with your children can no doubt bring joy and delight (see p.148), it can be just as much fun to make savoury recipes together. And it is especially nice to make a meal together and then sit down to eat as a family.

Before starting any recipe, it's helpful to get all the ingredients lined up so everything you need is organised and ready to go. Even younger children can be given quick, easy tasks such as helping to find ingredients in the fridge and cupboard. As they get older they can practise their reading skills and budding maths enthusiasts can identify numbers, as well as help count and weigh measurements.

As you get started, encourage your children to have a go at adding, mixing and sprinkling various ingredients and as they get more confident they can take on bigger roles. Take a look at our sticker chart on p.10 which encourages them to try new things and build their skills up over time.

Grilled lemon chicken

I made this recipe all the time when my children were toddlers. I would cut the chicken into little pieces and they loved to squeeze the lemon. Now that they are older they like to help me pound the chicken into flat pieces, the thinner the better.

Serves
a family of 4 or
6 children

Prep time
5 minutes plus
marinating

Cook time
10–15 minutes

Ingredients

4 boneless, skinless free-range chicken breasts

Juice of 1 lemon

1 garlic clove, finely chopped

2 tablespoons white wine

2 tablespoons extra virgin olive oil

Method

1. Place one chicken breast between two pieces of cling film, put it on a chopping board and pound with a rolling pin or meat tenderiser to make it as thin as possible. Repeat with the remaining chicken.

2. Combine the other ingredients in a shallow glass dish and stir well. Add the chicken, cover and set aside to marinate for at least 30 minutes or ideally overnight.

3. Remove the chicken from the marinade and place on a heated grill or frying pan. Cook on each side for 4–6 minutes until cooked through. Serve hot or at room temperature with lemon wedges on the side.

I can help pound the meat to make it as flat and thin as possible. I always remember to wash my hands well after touching raw chicken

Sweet potatoes with feta and pecans

This recipe has a nice combination of flavours and is a great side dish for Grilled lemon chicken (p.53) or Slow-cooked shoulder of lamb (p.93).

Serves
a family of 4 or
6 children

Prep time
10–15 minutes

Cook time
35 minutes

Ingredients

1kg sweet potatoes (3–5 sweet potatoes, depending on size)

2 tablespoons olive oil

40g pecan nuts

3 spring onions, roughly chopped

2 tablespoons coriander, roughly chopped

70g feta, crumbled

Sea salt and freshly ground pepper (optional)

Red chilli flakes (optional for grown-ups)

Method

1. Preheat the oven to 200°C/gas mark 6

2. Cut sweet potatoes into 2cm cubes and spread them out on a parchment-lined baking tray. Make sure the potatoes are in a single layer so they roast properly (use 2 trays if needed). Drizzle with the olive oil, season with salt and pepper and toss well with your hands.

3. Roast in the oven for 30–35 minutes until tender and browned (or a little longer depending on your oven). Turn over half way through cooking.

4. On a separate baking tray, roast the pecans for 5 minutes. Remove from the oven, let cool and roughly chop.

5. When the potatoes are ready, remove from oven and gently toss with chopped spring onions, coriander and pecans. Sprinkle on the feta, and chilli flakes if using, and serve immediately or at room temperature.

I can help toss the sweet potatoes in the olive oil with my hands and sprinkle the feta on top at the end

Sautéed spinach with garlic

Serves
a family of 4 or 6 children

Prep time
5 minutes

Cook time
5 minutes

Ingredients

1 tablespoon butter

1 tablespoon olive oil

4 cloves of garlic, minced

400g fresh spinach, washed

Sea salt

Freshly ground pepper

Wedge of lemon

Method

1. Melt butter and olive oil in a large pot over medium heat. Add garlic and sauté for 1–2 minutes, being careful not to let it brown.

2. Add spinach and stir so that it is covered in the oil. Turn heat to low and cover pot for a few minutes until spinach is wilted.

3. Remove cover and stir. Drain liquid from pan and season with salt, pepper and a squeeze of lemon. Serve immediately.

I can help squeeze the lemon on the spinach

Chicken curry

This recipe is very quick when you have leftover cooked chicken on hand from Simple roast chicken (p.63) or Homemade chicken stock (p.117)

Serves
a family of 4 or
6 children

Prep time
10 minutes

Cook time
20 minutes

Ingredients

1 tablespoon olive oil

1 large onion, finely chopped

2 garlic cloves, finely chopped

1 tablespoon finely chopped fresh root ginger

Pinch of chilli powder

2 teaspoons garam masala

400ml can coconut milk

175ml chicken stock

500g cooked free-range chicken, shredded

100g frozen peas

4 tablespoons coriander, finely chopped

Rice, to serve

Method

1. In a large pan, heat the oil and add the onion, garlic and ginger. Cook for 5 minutes over a medium heat. Add the chilli powder and garam masala and cook for a further 2 minutes.

2. Add the coconut milk and chicken stock. Bring to a simmer and cook for 5 minutes over a very low heat. Stir in the chicken and peas and simmer for a further 5 minutes. Stir in the fresh coriander and serve with rice.

I can help measure out the spices

Chicken stir-fry

Serves
a family of 4 or
6 children

Prep time
10 minutes

Cook time
8 minutes

Ingredients

1 tablespoon honey

2 tablespoons soy sauce

2 tablespoons rice wine vinegar

2 tablespoons cold pressed sunflower oil

1 mild red chilli, finely chopped (optional)

2 garlic cloves, finely chopped

8 spring onions, finely sliced

300g boneless, skinless free-range chicken breast, chopped into small pieces

100g broccoli florets, chopped into small pieces

2 medium carrots, cut into sticks

1 red pepper, de-seeded and chopped

300g pre-cooked egg noodles

1 tablespoon sesame seeds

Sesame oil, for drizzling

Method

1. In a small bowl mix together the honey, soy sauce and rice wine vinegar.

2. Heat a wok or a deep-sided frying pan over a medium heat. Add half the sunflower oil. When hot, add the chilli, garlic, spring onions and chicken. Stir-fry for 3–4 minutes. Tip the mixture out onto a plate and wipe the wok clean with kitchen paper.

3. Add the remaining oil and when hot, add the broccoli, carrots and red pepper and stir-fry for a further 2 minutes.

4. Add the chicken mixture and stir-fry for a further minute until the chicken is heated right through. Stir through the noodles, sprinkle over the sesame seeds and a drizzle of sesame oil. Serve immediately.

I can help prepare and measure out the ingredients in advance so everything is ready to be cooked

Chicken pie

Chicken pie is a favourite with my children who love pastry of any kind. Sometimes the pie filling will bubble over onto the baking sheet, so line it first with foil for easy clean-up.

Serves

a family of 4 with leftovers or 8 children

Prep time
30 minutes

Cook time
30–40 minutes

I can help shred the cooled cooked chicken and put it in the baking dish

Ingredients

4 x 150g boneless, skinless free-range chicken breasts

480ml reduced-salt chicken stock

1 tablespoon olive oil

1 large onion, finely chopped

1 leek, thinly sliced

2 carrots, chopped

60g unsalted butter

60g plain flour

360ml milk

½ teaspoon dried thyme

200g peas

2 tablespoons roughly chopped fresh flat-leaf parsley (optional)

Sheet ready-rolled puff pastry

Method

1. Preheat the oven to 200°C/gas mark 6.

2. Put the chicken and stock into a saucepan over a medium heat. Cover, bring to a simmer and cook for 8–10 minutes until the chicken is cooked through. Transfer the chicken to a separate bowl, reserving the liquid in a measuring jug to add to the sauce later.

3. Heat the oil in the same pan, add the onion, leek and carrots and sauté until soft, about 8 minutes. While the vegetables are cooking, shred the chicken into small pieces and put them into a 22cm x 22cm baking dish. When the vegetables are ready, add them to the dish and stir well.

4. Add the butter to the same pan and melt it over a low heat. Add the flour, stir well and cook for 1 minute. Gradually whisk in the chicken stock from the measuring jug (about 460ml), the milk and thyme. Bring to the boil, then turn down the heat and simmer, stirring until the sauce thickens enough to coat the spoon – another 1–2 minutes. Pour the sauce over the chicken and vegetables, add the peas and parsley and stir well to combine.

5. Lay the pastry sheet over the top, stretching it a bit if necessary, and trim to fit, crimping the edges. Cut a few slits to vent the steam. Place the dish on a baking sheet and bake for 30–40 minutes until the crust is golden and the filling is bubbling.

Simple roast chicken

A perfect recipe for Sunday lunch, but easy enough for a weeknight dinner too. Children can help sprinkle herbs on the chicken before it goes in the oven.

Serves
a family of 4 with leftovers

Prep time
10 minutes plus resting time

Cook time
1 hour 25 minutes–1 hour 35 minutes

I can help put the lemon and onions inside the chicken and sprinkle on the herbs. I always remember to wash my hands well after touching raw chicken

Ingredients

1.6–1.9kg free-range chicken, giblets removed

2 onions

1 lemon

1 garlic bulb

4–6 sprigs of fresh thyme or rosemary (optional)

3 tablespoons olive oil

Sea salt and freshly ground black pepper

Method

1. Preheat the oven to 180°C/gas mark 4. Weigh the chicken and calculate the cooking time; allow 40 minutes per kg, plus 20 minutes.

2. Halve and peel 1 onion and halve the lemon; put the onion and lemon halves inside the chicken along with 2–3 sprigs of the herbs.

3. Slice the remaining unpeeled onion and separate the garlic cloves. Scatter the onion slices and garlic cloves (with skin on) over the base of a roasting tin and place the chicken on top. Spoon the olive oil over the skin and rub it in well. Strip the leaves from the remaining sprigs of herb; if using rosemary, chop the leaves. Sprinkle the herbs over the chicken, along with some sea salt and black pepper.

4. Roast in the oven for the calculated time. Test to see if the chicken is cooked by inserting a skewer into the thickest part of the thigh: the juices should run clear.

5. Transfer the cooked chicken to a warm plate, cover with foil and set aside to rest for 15–20 minutes before carving and serving.

Brown rice pilaf

This pilaf is made with brown rice, which not only has more fibre than white rice, but gives this dish a lovely nutty flavour. Children can help break apart the broccoli florets before they are cooked and sprinkle on the pine nuts at the end.

Serves

a family of 4
or 6 children,
as a side dish

Prep time
5 minutes

Cook time
20 minutes
(plus rice cook
time)

Ingredients

225g brown rice

200g bite-size broccoli florets

2 tablespoons olive oil

1 onion, grated

2 garlic cloves, minced

100g chestnut mushrooms, chopped

100ml white wine

Juice of ½ lemon

50g toasted pine nuts

Sea salt and freshly ground black pepper (optional)

Method

1. Cook the rice according to the packet instructions.

2. Cook the broccoli in a large pan of boiling water for 2-3 minutes or until just tender. Drain and run under cold water to stop the cooking. Set aside.

3. Meanwhile, heat a large frying pan and add the olive oil. When hot add the onion and garlic and cook for 5 minutes. Add the mushrooms and cook for a further 5 minutes or until all the cooking juices have evaporated.

4. Add the white wine and lemon juice and allow it to bubble for 2 minutes to allow the alcohol to evaporate.

5. Add the broccoli and rice to the pan and cook, stirring frequently until the rice is piping hot. Stir in the pine nuts and season with salt and pepper. Serve straight away.

I can help separate the broccoli into small florets and sprinkle on the pine nuts

Glazed carrots

Serves
a family of 4 or
6 children

Prep time
5 minutes

Cook time
40 minutes

Ingredients

500g carrots, cut into batons

2 tablespoons olive oil

1 tablespoon orange juice

2 teaspoons maple syrup

Sea salt and freshly ground black pepper (optional)

Method

1. Preheat the oven to 190°C/gas mark 5.

2. Put the carrots into a medium roasting tin. Add the oil and season. Toss well to coat the carrots in the oil. Roast for 30 minutes.

3. Remove from the oven and stir in the orange juice and drizzle over the maple syrup. Roast for a further 10 minutes or until the carrots are cooked and golden.

Roasted vegetables

Serves
a family of 4 or
6 children

Prep time
10 minutes

Cook time
35–45 minutes

Ingredients

3 red onions, quartered

350g sliced butternut squash

2 red peppers, de-seeded and thickly sliced

2 courgettes, cut into 1cm pieces

Olive oil, for drizzling

Sea salt and freshly ground black pepper (optional)

Method

1. Preheat the oven to 200°C/gas mark 6.

2. Put all the vegetables into a large roasting tin, toss in a little olive oil so the vegetables are just covered and season with a little salt and black pepper.

3. Place in the oven for 35–45 minutes until cooked and tender.

Steamed broccoli trees

Serves
a family of 4 or
6 children

Prep time
5 minutes

Cook time
5 minutes

Ingredients

500g broccoli

½ lemon

1 teaspoon toasted sesame seeds

Method

1. Break the broccoli into small florets. Make sure they are all the same size so they cook evenly.

2. Put the florets into a steamer or colander and put on top of a pan of boiling water. Make sure the steamer or colander sits comfortably in the pan but does not touch the boiling water. Cover the steamer or colander with foil or a tight-fitting lid. Steam for 3–4 minutes or until the broccoli is just tender.

3. Tip the broccoli into a serving dish, squeeze over the lemon and finish by scattering over the sesame seeds.

I can help squeeze the lemon juice and sprinkle on the sesame seeds

Easy fish in foil

This is an easy recipe that doesn't leave your kitchen smelling like fish. You can prepare ahead and leave the parcel of foil in the fridge for up to two days (as long as the fish is within its use-by date). Just take it out 15–20 minutes before cooking. It's easy to double or triple the quantity if you are feeding a bigger group.

Serves
2–4 children
(smaller children
can share
one fillet)

Prep time
5 minutes

Cook time
12–15 minutes

Ingredients

2 tablespoons olive oil

2 x 125–150g fish fillets, eg salmon, haddock, cod or halibut, skin on

1 garlic clove, finely chopped

Sprigs of fresh herbs, eg rosemary or thyme

½ lemon, for squeezing

Method

1. Preheat the oven to 220°C/gas mark 7.

2. Take two pieces of foil and place one on top of the other (using two pieces helps ensure there are no leaks). Brush ½ tablespoon of the oil on the top layer of the foil. Check the fillets for bones, rinse with cold water, pat dry and place skin-side down on the foil. Rub the remaining oil into the fish. Top the fish with the chopped garlic and herbs and then squeeze some lemon juice over the top.

3. Close the foil, leaving a little air in the parcel, and place the parcel on a baking tray. Bake for 12–15 minutes, being careful not to overcook. To test, open the parcel after 12 minutes, the fish is cooked when it is opaque all the way through. If not, reseal the parcel and cook for another 2–3 minutes. To serve, remove the skin from the fish and drizzle over any cooking juices.

I can help sprinkle the garlic and herbs and wrap the fish in foil parcels

Tartare sauce

This sauce is great with Fish in foil (opposite), Fish fingers (p.127) and the Salmon 'burgers' (p.104).

Serves
a family of 4

Prep time
5 minutes

Ingredients

3 tablespoons Greek yoghurt

3 tablespoons mayonnaise

½ teaspoon horseradish

Juice of ½ lemon

4 teaspoons small capers

Method

Mix all the ingredients in a small bowl.

Fish pie

Serves

a family of 4 or
6 children

Prep time
30 minutes

Cook time
35 minutes

Ingredients

5 medium potatoes, cut into
even-sized chunks

Knob of butter

3–4 tablespoons milk

2 x 150g cod fillets, skinned, boned
and cut into large chunks

2 x 150g salmon fillets, skinned,
boned and cut into large chunks

75g baby spinach

For the cheese sauce

30g unsalted butter

30g plain flour

400ml milk

90g Cheddar cheese, grated

Pinch of grated nutmeg

Sea salt and freshly ground black
pepper (optional)

Method

1. Preheat the oven to 180°C/gas mark 4.

2. Cook the potatoes in a pan of boiling water for about 15 minutes or until
tender, then drain and mash with the butter and milk.

3. Meanwhile, make the cheese sauce, melt the butter in a medium pan over
a medium heat and whisk in the flour until smooth. Slowly whisk in the
milk, stirring constantly, so it doesn't become lumpy. When all the milk
has been added, bring to the boil then turn the heat down and simmer,
continuing to stir until the sauce is thick enough to coat the spoon or
whisk. Stir in most of the cheese (reserving a little for the topping) and
stir for a further 2 minutes until the cheese has melted and the sauce is
thick and smooth. Add the nutmeg and season to taste.

4. Gently stir the fish and baby spinach into the cheese sauce and transfer it
to a baking dish. Spoon the mashed potato on top and sprinkle with the
reserved cheese. Place on a baking tray and bake for 35 minutes or until
the cheese is bubbling and golden brown.

*Tips: Cover with cling film and freeze before cooking, once you have assembled
the pie. To cook straight from frozen, cook as above for 45–50 minutes. Check the
pie is piping hot in the centre before serving.*

*I can help
spoon the
mashed potato
onto the pie
and sprinkle
on the cheese
before it goes
in the oven*

Salmon teriyaki

The flavours in this dish are really child friendly. Children can help make the marinade by measuring the various ingredients and whisking them together before it goes on the stove.

Serves
a family of 4 or
6 children

Prep time
10 minutes plus
marinating

Cook time
7–10 minutes

Ingredients

3 tablespoons soy sauce

2 tablespoons mirin

2 tablespoons clear honey

1 teaspoon finely grated fresh root ginger

4 x 130–160g salmon fillets, skinned

2 tablespoons fresh coriander, chopped (optional)

Brown rice and edamame beans, to serve

Method

1. Place the soy sauce, mirin, honey, ginger and 3 tablespoons of water in a small pan and whisk together. Bring to the boil and gently simmer over a medium heat for 2 minutes.

2. Pour the marinade into a shallow glass dish and leave to cool. Add the salmon fillets, cover and marinate in the fridge for at least 1 hour or overnight.

3. Preheat the grill to high. Place the salmon on a baking tray, reserving the marinade, and cook for 7–10 minutes until golden.

4. Meanwhile put the reserved marinade into a small pan and bring to the boil, then remove from the heat.

5. Drizzle the salmon with the reduced marinade and garnish with coriander. Serve with brown rice and edamame beans.

I can help measure the ingredients and whisk them all together

Prawns with pesto

My children love this recipe and it is a really quick and easy weekday supper if the pesto is already made ahead and in the fridge (or store bought). Serve tossed with pasta or on top of brown rice with a vegetable on the side.

Serves
a family of 4 or
6 children

Prep time
5 minutes

Cook time
4–6 minutes

Ingredients

2 tablespoons olive oil

300g peeled prawns

75g Pesto (p.78) or one pot shop-bought

Brown rice or pasta and vegetables, to serve

Method

1. Heat the olive oil in a medium non-stick frying pan. When the oil is hot, add the prawns and cook for 2–3 minutes on each side or until piping hot.

2. Remove from the heat and stir in the pesto. Serve with brown rice or pasta and vegetables.

I can help stir in the pesto

Pesto (with hidden kale)

This pesto is extra healthy and so good that children don't notice the hidden vegetable. Leftovers keep in the fridge for about a week.

Makes
350g pesto

Prep time
5 minutes

Ingredients

150g kale, stalks removed and roughly chopped

85g toasted pine nuts

30g basil leaves

2 garlic cloves

150ml olive oil plus extra to finish

Zest of ½ lemon

80g Parmesan cheese, grated

Sea salt and freshly ground black pepper

Method

1. Place the kale, pine nuts, basil, garlic, olive oil and lemon zest into a food processor and pulse to form a coarse paste.

2. Add the Parmesan and whiz again until the pesto is smooth. Taste and season if necessary and transfer into a glass or plastic container. Cover with a little more oil and store in the fridge for up to a week.

I can help pick the basil leaves off the stalks and add the ingredients to the food processor

Tomato sauce

This is a simple tomato sauce that works well with Beef meatballs (p.80) or with plain pasta on nights when you need something quick. It freezes well so you can double the recipe and put the leftovers in the freezer.

Serves
a family of 4 or
6 children

Prep time
5 minutes

Cook time
10–15 minutes

Ingredients

3 tablespoons olive oil

1 medium onion, chopped

4 garlic cloves, finely chopped

1 tablespoon dried mixed herbs

2 x 400g cans chopped tomatoes

Freshly ground black pepper

Method

1. Heat the olive oil in a saucepan over a medium-high heat. Add the onion, garlic and mixed herbs, stirring occasionally until soft, about 2–3 minutes. Add the tomatoes and bring to the boil.

2. Turn down to simmer, stirring occasionally, until the sauce thickens, about 10–15 minutes.

Tip: This freezes well for up to 1 month in an airtight container. Allow to cool to room temperature before freezing.

I can help measure out all the ingredients

Beef meatballs

Serves
a family of 4 or
6 children

Prep time
15 minutes

Cook time
10 minutes

Ingredients

4 tablespoons olive oil

1 onion, finely chopped

1 garlic clove, finely chopped

500g minced beef

50g chopped spinach

1 teaspoon dried mixed herbs

50g fresh breadcrumbs

1 medium free-range egg, beaten

Sea salt and freshly ground black pepper (optional)

Tomato sauce (p.79) and pasta, to serve

Method

1. Heat half of the olive oil in a large, deep-sided frying pan. Add the onion and garlic and cook for 5 minutes until soft and golden. Transfer to a large bowl and allow to cool.

2. Add the beef, chopped spinach, herbs, breadcrumbs, beaten egg and seasoning to the bowl and stir well, to combine. Using your hands, roll the mixture into 24 even-sized balls.

3. Heat the remaining oil in the frying pan over a medium heat and cook the meatballs for about 8–10 minutes, turning every couple of minutes.

4. Serve with Tomato sauce (p.79) and your favourite pasta.

I can help make the meatballs with my hands. I always remember to wash my hands well after touching raw meat

Aubergine bake

This is a nice vegetarian alternative and is usually popular with children who like lasagne. Little helpers can spoon on the tomato sauce and layer all the ingredients.

Serves
a family of 4 or
6 children

Prep time
25 minutes

Cook time
30–40 minutes

Ingredients

2 tablespoons olive oil

2 garlic cloves, finely chopped

2 x 400g cans chopped tomatoes

1 tablespoon dried mixed herbs

2 large aubergines

250g mozzarella cheese, sliced

50g Parmesan cheese, grated

Sea salt and freshly ground black pepper (optional)

Method

1. Preheat the oven to 180°C/gas mark 4.

2. Heat half of the olive oil in a medium saucepan, add the garlic and gently cook for 2 minutes. Add the tomatoes and mixed herbs and simmer for 15 minutes or until the sauce thickens.

3. Meanwhile, slice the aubergines into 1cm thick rounds. Brush both sides with the remaining oil and sauté in a non-stick frying pan over a low to medium heat, turning a few times until very soft (about 5 minutes each side). It's important to get the aubergine as tender as possible, so take extra time if needed.

4. Season the tomato sauce, to taste. Spread a few spoonfuls of sauce across the bottom of an ovenproof dish. Place about a third of the aubergines in a layer over the sauce. Cover with a layer of mozzarella (again, about a third) and sprinkle with Parmesan cheese. Repeat twice more, and end with a thin layer of sauce. Cover with the remaining Parmesan and bake for 30–40 minutes until bubbling.

I can help layer the aubergine slices, mozzarella and tomato sauce

Bow tie pasta with sausages, tomato & rosemary

This recipe is quick, tasty and loved by kids. Older children can squeeze the sausage out of the casings and younger ones can help sprinkle on the Parmesan cheese at the end. We've used farfalle pasta here but fusilli and penne both work well.

Serves
a family of 4 or
6 children

Prep time
5 minutes

Cook time
20–25 minutes

Ingredients

2 tablespoons olive oil

450g organic sausages, casing removed

2 garlic cloves, finely chopped

1 large sprig of rosemary, leaves removed and finely chopped

1 tablespoon dried mixed herbs

2 x 400g cans chopped tomatoes

400g pasta, eg farfalle, penne or fusilli

2 tablespoons grated Parmesan cheese

Method

1. Heat the oil in a large frying pan over a medium heat. Remove the sausages from their casings and add to the pan, breaking up with a fork. Cook until browned for about 5–7 minutes.

2. Add the garlic, rosemary and mixed herbs and cook for a further 1 minute. Add the chopped tomatoes and bring to the boil.

3. Meanwhile, cook the pasta in a large pan of salted water for 10 minutes or according to the packet instructions. Drain, and return to the pan.

4. Stir the sauce into the pasta and serve topped with grated Parmesan.

I can help squeeze the sausages out of the casings and sprinkle on the Parmesan cheese

Turkey Bolognese

Minced turkey is sold in most UK supermarkets. I use it in Bolognese, Lasagne (p.88) and Burgers (p.98) when my kids need a break from red meat. If you're after a more traditional Bolognese, replace the turkey with beef mince, or a combination of beef and pork mince works well also.

Serves
a family of 4 with leftovers or 6–8 children

Prep time
10 minutes

Cook time
1–3 hours

Ingredients

3 tablespoons olive oil

1 onion, chopped

1 carrot, chopped

1 courgette, chopped

2 tablespoons dried mixed herbs

3 garlic cloves, finely chopped

500g minced turkey

2 x 400g cans chopped tomatoes

Freshly ground black pepper

Spaghetti or tagliatelle and Parmesan cheese, to serve

Method

1. Heat 2 tablespoons of the olive oil in a large, heavy-based pan or flameproof casserole dish over a medium heat. Add the onion, carrot and courgette and sauté until softened but not browned, about 6 minutes.

2. Add the mixed herbs and garlic and cook for 2–3 more minutes. Tip the mixture into a bowl, wipe the pan and add the remaining oil.

3. Add the minced turkey, breaking it up with a fork or a wooden spoon to make sure there are no big lumps of mince. Cook over a medium heat until the mince starts to brown, about 5–7 minutes.

4. Add the cooked vegetable mixture and tomatoes to the mince and bring to the boil. Reduce the heat to low so the sauce continues to simmer, for at least 1 hour and up to 3 hours.

5. Serve the sauce over pasta and topped with Parmesan cheese.

Tip: The sauce can be frozen for up to 2 months in an airtight container. Allow to cool to room temperature before freezing.

I can help measure out ingredients and break the mince up with a wooden spoon

Lasagne

This recipe uses the Turkey Bolognese recipe from p.87 as the meat sauce. As with the Bolognese, the turkey can be replaced with the meat of your choosing.

Serves
6 people

Prep time
30–40 minutes

Cook time
45–55 minutes

Ingredients

Meat sauce as on p.87

60g unsalted butter

60g plain flour

1 litre milk

125g Cheddar cheese, grated

Freshly ground black pepper

Large pinch of grated nutmeg

8 sheets of lasagne

200g spinach

50g mozzarella cheese, grated

2 tablespoons grated Parmesan cheese

Method

1. Preheat the oven to 180°C/gas mark 4.

2. Follow the recipe on p.87 to make the meat sauce.

3. To make the cheese sauce, melt the butter in a saucepan over a medium heat and whisk in the flour until smooth, stirring continuously. Slowly whisk in the milk, stirring constantly. When all the milk has been added, bring to the boil, and continue to boil for 2 minutes, stirring constantly with a wooden spoon. Turn the sauce down to a simmer and cook until the sauce is thick and coats the back of the spoon. Stir in the cheese, season with black pepper and nutmeg.

4. To assemble the lasagne, spoon one third of the meat into the bottom of a baking dish. Top with half the lasagne sheets, another third of the meat, half the spinach, and half the cheese sauce. Add the remaining lasagne sheets, then the rest of the meat, spinach and cheese sauce. Sprinkle the mozzarella and grated Parmesan cheese on top. Place the dish on a baking tray and bake for 45–55 minutes.

I can help layer the meat, pasta, spinach and cheese sauce to assemble the lasagne

Lamb and lentils

This is an easy recipe to put together and children can help you measure out the ingredients. It cooks in just over an hour in the oven, which is handy when you want to do the prep work in advance.

Serves
a family of 4 or
6 children

Prep time
20 minutes

Cook time
1 hour and
15 minutes

Ingredients

2 tablespoons olive oil

1 onion, finely chopped

1 leek, chopped

500g minced lamb

2 garlic cloves, finely chopped

1 tablespoon dried mixed herbs

2 carrots, diced

300g butternut squash and sweet potato, cubed

400g can chopped tomatoes

150g red lentils

500ml lamb, chicken or vegetable stock

Method

1. Heat the olive oil in a medium flameproof casserole dish over a medium heat. Add the onion, leek, lamb, garlic and herbs and cook until the meat is browned, breaking the mince up with a wooden spoon. Add the remaining ingredients and bring to the boil. Stir and cover.

2. Cook in the oven for 1 hour and 15 minutes or until the lentils and vegetables are tender.

I can help measure out all the ingredients and add them to the casserole dish

Roasted cauliflower

I was never a fan of cauliflower until I discovered how good it tastes roasted. Sometimes we add it to cooked quinoa with some crumbled feta and pine nuts, which is really delicious.

Serves
a family of 4 or
6 children

Prep time
5–10 minutes

Cook time
30–35 minutes

Ingredients

2 tablespoons olive oil plus extra for greasing

1 cauliflower, broken into bite-sized florets

Salt and freshly ground black pepper (optional)

Method

1. Preheat the oven to 200°C/gas mark 6.

2. Lightly oil a large roasting tin or baking tray. Place the cauliflower florets in a large bowl. Add the olive oil, salt and pepper and toss well to coat. Spread the florets out in a single layer in the tin or on the tray.

3. Roast the cauliflower for 30–35 minutes, or until the tops are light brown and the cauliflower is tender when pricked with a fork. Serve immediately.

I can help break up the cauliflower into florets and toss them in olive oil with my hands

Slow-cooked shoulder of lamb

This makes a great Sunday lunch or weekend family supper. Children can help rub on the rosemary and garlic.

Serves
a family of 4 plus leftovers

Prep time
5 minutes

Cook time
3 hours

Ingredients

15 garlic cloves (10 left whole and 5 finely chopped)

6 sprigs of rosemary

1 whole shoulder of lamb, bone-in (about 2kg)

1 tablespoon finely chopped rosemary

Sea salt and freshly ground black pepper (optional)

Method

1. Preheat the oven to 220°C/gas mark 7.

2. Put the whole garlic cloves and the sprigs of rosemary in a lidded, ovenproof dish large enough to hold the joint or a roasting tin. Place the lamb on top of the rosemary and garlic. Rub the crushed garlic and the finely chopped rosemary over the lamb and season with a little salt and pepper. Tightly cover the dish with foil and then put the lid or cover the tin with a double layer of foil.

3. Place the lamb in the oven, reduce the temperature to 170°C/gas mark 3 and cook for 3 hours.

I can help rub the garlic and rosemary over the lamb. I always remember to wash my hands well after touching raw meat

Lamb and barley hotpot

This recipe is easy to assemble because you don't need to brown the meat. It's a good recipe when you want to do the prepping in advance and have a lovely family meal emerge from the oven a couple of hours later.

Serves
a family of 4 or 6 children

Prep time
10 minutes

Cook time
2–2½ hours

Ingredients

700g lamb shoulder or neck fillet, trimmed and cut into bite-size pieces

3 large red potatoes (about 500g), medium sliced

2 onions, sliced into medium rings

1–2 sprigs of fresh thyme, leaves stripped

360ml lamb or beef stock

2 tablespoons pearl barley

freshly ground black pepper

Method

1. Preheat the oven to 170°C/gas mark 3.

2. In a medium casserole dish, arrange the lamb, potatoes and onion in layers, a third of the mixture for each, seasoning each layer with freshly ground pepper. Finish with a top layer of potatoes. Sprinkle the fresh thyme leaves on top, pour in the stock and sprinkle over the pearl barley.

3. Put the lid on the casserole and cook in the oven for 2–2½ hours or until the meat is tender and the sauce is thickened.

I can help layer the lamb and potatoes and sprinkle on the herbs

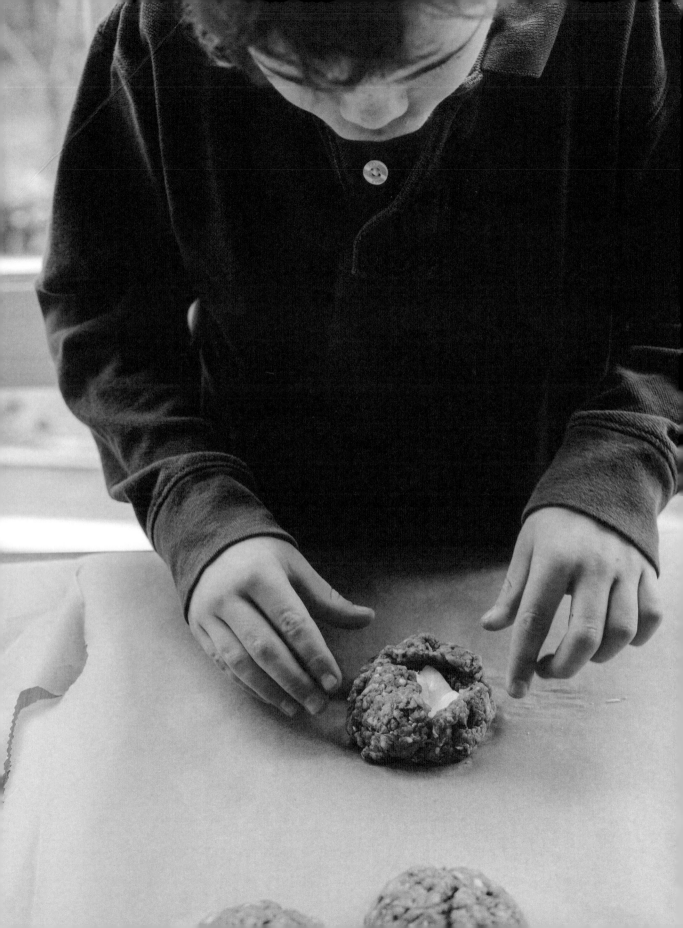

Beefburgers with a surprise in the middle

My children love burgers. In this book we have several versions: beef, turkey (p.98), lamb (p.103) and even salmon (p.104). In this beef burger recipe we've added some grated courgette which went down well with our testers. Children can help form the meat mixture into patties and insert the mozzarella 'surprise'.

Makes
8 small burgers

Prep time
15 minutes

Cook time
10 minutes

Ingredients

1 courgette, grated and excess water squeezed out

500g lean minced beef

2 garlic cloves, finely chopped

1 teaspoon dried oregano

1 teaspoon sun-dried tomato purée

8 mini mozzarella balls or 125g mozzarella cut into 8 equal pieces

Cold pressed sunflower oil for frying

Salt and freshly ground black pepper (optional)

To serve

Mini burger buns, lettuce leaves, sliced tomatoes, sliced red onion, sliced avocado

I can help form the meat into burgers and insert the mozzarella surprise. I always remember to wash my hands well after touching raw meat

Method

1. Place the courgette, beef, garlic, oregano and sun-dried tomato purée in a large bowl. Season and, using your hands, mix all the ingredients together to combine.

2. Divide the mixture into 8 even-sized balls and flatten with the palm of your hand. Place a mozzarella ball or piece in the middle of each patty and reshape the balls so the cheese is hidden in the middle of the burger.

3. Brush a large non-stick frying pan with oil and cook the burgers on a low heat for about 5 minutes on each side – cook in batches if they don't all fit in one pan.

4. Serve the burgers in mini buns, with lettuce, sliced tomatoes, red onion rings and slices of avocado.

Turkey burgers

Makes

8 small burgers or
4 regular burgers

Prep time

5 minutes plus 15
minutes chilling

Cook time

8–12 minutes

Ingredients

50g fresh breadcrumbs

75ml full-fat milk

500g minced turkey

¼ teaspoon freshly ground black pepper

20g unsalted butter

Method

1. Combine all the ingredients, except the butter, by hand in a bowl. Divide into 8 mini burgers or 4 regular-sized burgers. Let them stand for 15 minutes.

2. Heat the butter in a saucepan over a medium heat until it bubbles and starts to brown. Add the burgers and cook for 4–6 minutes on each side or until they are brown and crisp and the centres are cooked through.

Tip: Add grated carrot or finely chopped cooked spinach to include some hidden veg.

I can help mix all the ingredients together in the bowl and shape the meat into burgers. I always remember to wash my hands well after touching raw meat

Sweet potato chips

Serves

a family of 4 or
6 children

Prep time

10 minutes

Cook time

25–30 minutes

Ingredients

3 sweet potatoes (unpeeled)

1–2 tablespoons olive oil

2 teaspoons flour

Method

1. Preheat the oven to 200°C/gas mark 6. Place two baking trays in the oven to preheat.

2. Cut each potato lengthwise into eight equal pieces, and then cut again lengthwise into wedges so they are all approximately the same size.

3. Put the wedges into a large bowl and toss them in enough olive oil that they are just coated.

4. Place the wedges onto the baking sheets and sprinkle on the flour. Toss again and spread out making sure that they aren't touching. Bake in the oven for 25–30 minutes, turning once half way through cooking.

5. Serve with ketchup.

I can help toss the sweet potato wedges in the olive oil

Homemade tzatziki

Serves

a family of 4 or
6 children

Prep time

5–10 minutes

Ingredients

8 tablespoons Greek yoghurt

½ cucumber, grated or finely diced, excess liquid squeezed out

1 garlic clove, finely chopped

1 tablespoon finely chopped fresh mint

1 tablespoon olive oil

Method

Mix all the ingredients in a bowl and set aside to serve with Lamb burgers (p.103) or Homemade chorizo (p.136)

I can help grate the cucumber and squeeze out the liquid

Lamb burgers

Makes

8 small burgers or
4 regular burgers

Prep time

15 minutes plus
chilling

Cook time

10–15 minutes

Ingredients

500g minced lamb

½ teaspoon ground cumin

½ teaspoon ground coriander

1 onion, grated

2 garlic cloves, finely chopped

2 tablespoons finely chopped fresh mint

2 tablespoons finely chopped fresh coriander

Pitta bread, tzatziki (p.101) and cucumber slices, to serve

Method

1. Mix all the ingredients together in a large bowl. Divide into 8 mini burgers or 4 regular ones, wet your hands and roll each ball into an oval shape. Place onto a baking tray and place in the fridge for 30 minutes.

2. Cook the burgers on a griddle pan or in a frying pan for 3–4 minutes each side. (Or 5–6 minutes per side if you are making 4 larger burgers.) Serve with warmed pitta bread, Homemade tzatziki (p.101) and cucumber slices.

I can help mix the ingredients together in a bowl and shape the meat into burgers. I always remember to wash my hands well after touching raw meat

Salmon 'burgers'

I don't serve these on buns, but the burger shape helped pique my children's interest in these very tasty salmon quinoa cakes. Quinoa is a great source of protein and a good alternative to potato. You can use plain quinoa or the red & white quinoa which gives these a lovely colour.

Makes

4 'burgers'

Prep time

15 minutes plus 1 hour chilling

Cook time

10 minutes

Ingredients

100g cooked quinoa

150g cooked salmon, boned, skinned and flaked

100g smoked salmon, finely chopped

Juice of ½ lemon

2 spring onions, finely sliced

2 tablespoons finely chopped fresh mint

1 medium free-range egg

1½ tablespoons plain flour

2 tablespoons cold pressed sunflower oil for frying

Salt and freshly ground black pepper (optional)

Method

1. Line a baking tray with greaseproof paper.

2. In a large bowl, mix together all the ingredients except the oil.

3. Divide the mixture into 4 even-sized patties. Place on the lined tray and chill in the fridge for 1 hour.

4. Heat the oil in a large non-stick frying pan and cook the fishcakes over a medium heat for 5 minutes on each side or until golden brown and cooked through.

5. Serve on their own or with a side vegetable.

I can help mix the ingredients together in a bowl and shape the burgers

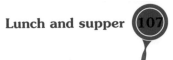

Easy pitta pizzas

This recipe is fun for a play date or a larger group. Children can spread on the tomato purée and choose their own toppings.

Makes

4 mini pizzas

Prep time

5 minutes

Cook time

12 minutes

Ingredients

3 tablespoons tomato purée

4 pitta breads (I use brown but white also works)

150g mozzarella cheese, grated

Large pinch of dried oregano

1 tablespoon olive oil

Suggested toppings: chopped spinach, sautéed mushrooms, cut up Parma ham, olives, whatever your children fancy

Method

1. Preheat the oven to 220°C/gas mark 7.

2. Mix the tomato purée with 3 tablespoons of water. Place the pitta breads on a baking tray and spread the tomato mixture over the top, add your chosen toppings, scatter over the cheese and oregano.

3. Drizzle with the olive oil and bake in the oven for 10–12 minutes

I can help spread the tomato purée on the pittas and add my favourite toppings

Leek and potato frittata

This recipe makes a great lunch or picnic. It can be served hot or made in advance and served at room temperature. You'll need 6 eggs which children can take turns cracking.

Serves
a family of 4 or
6 children

Prep time
10 minutes

Cook time
10–15 minutes

Ingredients

2 tablespoons olive oil

1 potato, finely diced

1 leek, chopped

6 medium free-range eggs

100g Cheddar cheese, grated

2 tablespoons roughly chopped fresh flat-leaf parsley (optional)

Salt and freshly ground black pepper (optional)

Salad, to serve

Method

1. Heat half the oil in a non-stick frying pan and sauté the diced potato over a medium heat until golden. Transfer the potato to a plate lined with kitchen paper.

2. Add the remaining oil and the chopped leek to the pan. Fry over a gentle heat for 5 minutes.

3. Meanwhile, in a separate bowl, beat the eggs, then mix in the cheese and parsley (if using). Season.

4. Preheat the grill to high.

5. Return the potatoes to the pan and pour over the egg mixture. Cook over a medium-low heat for about 5–8 minutes until the bottom of the frittata is cooked through but the top still runny.

6. Place the frittata under the grill for 5 minutes or until the top is brown and the centre is cooked through.

7. Remove, leave to cool for 2 minutes, then cut into slices and serve with salad.

Variation: Add 90g of diced, cooked chorizo to the egg mixture.

I can help crack the eggs

Chicken bites with a cornflake crust

This recipe is our version of healthy chicken nuggets. The cornflakes make a great, crunchy coating and children love to help crush the cornflakes. A good trick is to put the cornflakes in a plastic freezer bag and roll a rolling pin over it a few times. Or even squash with your hands.

Serves
a family of 4 or
6 children

Prep time
15 minutes

Cook time
12 minutes

Ingredients

2 tablespoons plain flour

1 medium free-range egg, beaten

100g cornflakes (preferably sugar-free)

1 teaspoon paprika

1 tablespoon grated Parmesan cheese

500g boneless, skinless free-range chicken breasts, cut into 2 x 4cm pieces

Method

1. Preheat the oven to 200°C/gas mark 6. Line a baking tray with baking parchment.

2. Put the flour onto one large plate and the egg in a shallow bowl. Place the cornflakes in a separate bowl and crush lightly with the back of a spoon. Don't crush them too much or they won't have any texture. Stir in the paprika and Parmesan.

3. Dip the chicken pieces first into the flour, then egg and then the cornflake mixture. Place onto the lined baking tray. Bake for 10–12 minutes.

I can help crush the cornflakes and dip the chicken pieces in the egg mixture and cornflake crumbs. I always remember to wash my hands well after touching raw chicken

Green pie

This pie can be served on its own as a light meal or in smaller portions as a side dish.

Serves
a family of 4 with leftovers or
8 children

Prep time
20–25 minutes

Cook time
1 hour and
5 minutes

Ingredients

100g unsalted butter, melted plus extra for greasing

2 tablespoons olive oil

2 medium onions, sliced

280g frozen spinach

6 sheets filo pastry (about 270g)

6 medium free-range eggs, beaten

Large pinch of grated nutmeg

50g grated Parmesan cheese

40g fresh, white breadcrumbs

200g feta cheese, crumbled

Freshly ground black pepper

Method

1. Preheat the oven to 190°C/gas mark 5. Butter a non-stick 24cm ovenproof pie dish.

2. Warm the olive oil in a medium pan over a medium heat. Cook the onions for 10–15 minutes, until they are slightly browned. Season with pepper and set aside to cool.

3. In a large pan sauté half the spinach over a medium heat, for 2 minutes. Transfer to a colander and repeat with the remaining spinach.

4. Place a sheet of filo pastry in the pie dish, letting the edges hang over the side. Brush with melted butter and repeat with the remaining sheets to line the dish, reserving a little of the butter.

5. Squeeze the spinach to get rid of as much liquid as possible. In a bowl combine the spinach with the onions, eggs, nutmeg, Parmesan, breadcrumbs and feta. Put the mixture in the middle of the pastry and fold the edges over the top to seal in the filling.

6. Brush the top of the pie with the remaining melted butter and bake for 1 hour, until the top is golden and the filling set. Allow to cool before serving.

I can help by brushing the pastry with the melted butter

Chicken quesadillas

Quesadillas are a favourite with my children and we make them all the time for a quick, easy after-school supper. You can substitute the chicken with sautéed mushrooms and spinach if you want a veggie version.

Serves
a family of 4 or
8 children

Prep time
15 minutes

Cook time
8–12 minutes

Ingredients

1 ripe avocado, lightly mashed

2 tablespoons soured cream

Juice of 1 lime

200g Cheddar cheese, grated

250g cooked chicken, shredded

4 cherry tomatoes, roughly chopped

1 spring onion, finely sliced (optional)

1 small bunch coriander leaves, roughly chopped (optional)

8 flour tortillas

Spray oil

Freshly ground black pepper

I can help stir the avocado mixture and layer the ingredients on to the quesadillas

Method

1. In a small bowl, place the avocado, soured cream and lime juice. Stir, cover and set aside.

2. In a large bowl, place the cheese, chicken, cherry tomatoes and spring onion and coriander, if using. Stir gently until everything is well combined. Season with a little black pepper.

3. Place 4 tortillas on the kitchen surface and divide the filling mixture equally between the tortillas, spreading it out in an even layer. Top with the remaining 4 tortillas.

4. Pour the oil into a large, non-stick frying pan over a medium heat.

5. Using a fish slice, transfer one of the quesadillas to the oiled frying pan and cook for 1–2 minutes. Carefully turn over and cook for another minute.

6. Transfer to a plate and cut into quarters. Repeat to cook the remaining quesadillas. Serve with the avocado mixture on the side.

Lentil soup

This soup freezes well if you want to make a double batch. Children can help you rinse the lentils and prepare the various ingredients.

Serves
a family of 4 with
leftovers or
8 children

Prep time
20 minutes

Cook time
30–35 minutes

Ingredients

2 tablespoons olive oil

1 large onion, chopped

1 large leek, chopped

2 medium carrots, chopped

1 red or yellow pepper, de-seeded and chopped

3 garlic cloves, finely chopped

400g can chopped tomatoes

1 bay leaf

1 teaspoon fresh thyme leaves

200g Puy lentils, rinsed

1.5 litres Homemade chicken stock (p.117) or store-bought

1½ teaspoons balsamic vinegar

Freshly ground black pepper

Method

1. Heat the olive oil in a medium heavy-based pan over a medium heat and add the onion, leek, carrots and pepper, cook, stirring occasionally, until the vegetables begin to soften, about 2 minutes. Add the garlic and cook for 1 minute. Stir in the tomatoes, bay leaf and thyme, cook for a further minute.

2. Stir in the lentils and season with pepper, cover, reduce the heat to medium-low, and cook until the vegetables have softened, 8 to 10 minutes.

3. Uncover, increase the heat to high and add the stock or water. Bring to the boil, then cover partially and reduce the heat to low. Simmer until the lentils are tender but still hold their shape, about 30 to 35 minutes. Discard the bay leaf.

4. Purée 700ml of the soup in a liquidiser or with a hand blender until smooth, then return to the pan. Stir in the balsamic vinegar and reheat the soup over a medium-low heat until piping hot.

Tip: This soup can be made in advance. After adding the vinegar, cool to room temperature and refrigerate for up to 2 days.

I can help rinse the lentils

Homemade chicken stock

This stock is easy to make and it is useful to have on hand in the fridge or freezer. It's also a good way to cook chicken which you can use in the Chicken curry recipe (p.56) or Chicken quesadillas (p.115).

Makes
2 litres

Prep time
20 minutes plus cooling

Cook time
2¾ hours

Ingredients

1–1.5kg whole free-range chicken, giblets removed and discarded

2 carrots, roughly chopped

1 onion, cut in half

1 leek, roughly chopped

2 garlic cloves

2 bay leaves

4 sprigs of fresh thyme

2 big pinches of salt (optional)

1 pinch of black peppercorns

Method

1. Put the chicken in a large pan and cover with a generous amount of cold water. Put a lid on the pan, bring to the boil, then turn the heat down to a simmer. Skim off any foam, using a slotted spoon, and add the vegetables, bay leaves, thyme, salt and peppercorns. Continue to simmer, uncovered, for 2 hours. Skim off any fat or foam as the stock cooks and if the liquid gets low, add a bit more water. Do not let it boil, just simmer.

2. Strain the stock into a large jug or bowl and set aside to cool to room temperature. Discard the vegetables and place the chicken carcass and any meat that has come off on a plate to cool for at least 10 minutes.

3. Remove the meat from the chicken and allow it to cool to room temperature. Cover and store the cooked chicken and the stock in the fridge for up to 2 days.

Tip: The stock freezes well for up to 2 months. Transfer to an airtight container and allow to cool to room temperature before freezing. Allow to defrost thoroughly before using.

Asian noodle soup

This soup is at its best made with Homemade chicken stock (p.117) but store-bought or even a stock cube work well too.

Serves
a family of 4
or 6 children

Prep time
10 minutes

Cook time
7 minutes

Ingredients

1 litre Homemade chicken stock (p.117)

2cm piece fresh root ginger, peeled and grated

2 garlic cloves, peeled and finely chopped

2 tablespoons soy sauce

100g cooked chicken, shredded

300g pack stir-fry vegetables

265g pack straight-to-wok noodles

2 spring onions, sliced

2 tablespoons fresh coriander, roughly chopped

1 lime, cut into wedges

Method

1. Put the stock, ginger, garlic and 1 tablespoon soy sauce in a medium pan and bring to a simmer. Simmer for 5 minutes.

2. Add the chicken, stir-fry vegetables and noodles, bring to the boil and simmer for a further 2 minutes.

3. Add the spring onions, coriander and lime wedges and drizzle with the remaining soy sauce. Serve immediately.

Tip: This soup is best eaten on the same day it is made while the vegetables still have their vibrant colour.

I can help shred the chicken and squeeze the lime at the end

Tomato soup

We often have this soup for lunch on cold, damp Saturdays when the children get home from football. I serve it with either cheese toasties or toasted pitta bread cut into soldiers for dipping. With a bit of supervision, older kids can help you purée the soup with a hand blender.

Serves

a family of 4 with leftovers or 8 children

Prep time
15 minutes

Cook time
40 minutes

Ingredients

2 tablespoons olive oil

1 onion, chopped

1 carrot, chopped

2 garlic cloves, finely chopped

3 x 400g cans chopped tomatoes

2 tablespoons tomato purée

1 litre Homemade chicken stock (p.117) or vegetable stock

2 tablespoons fresh basil, roughly torn (optional)

Method

1. In a large saucepan, heat the oil and cook the onion, carrot and garlic for 5 minutes, stirring occasionally.

2. Add the canned tomatoes and tomato purée and cook for a further 5 minutes. Add the stock and bring to the boil and reduce to a simmer for 30 minutes. Purée the soup, in batches in a liquidiser or with a hand blender until smooth.

Tip: This soup freezes well for up to 2 months in an airtight container. Allow to cool to room temperature before freezing. Reheat, from frozen, over a low heat until the soup is piping hot.

I can help purée with the hand blender

Chicken, pesto and mozzarella wraps

Makes

8 halves

Prep time

5 minutes

Ingredients

4 wholewheat or seeded tortillas

2 tablespoons Pesto (p.78 or use store-bought)

150g cooked chicken, shredded

125g mozzarella cheese, thinly sliced

50g spinach

Method

1. Place the tortillas on the kitchen surface and spread ½ tablespoon of pesto over each one. Top each with one-quarter of the shredded chicken and mozzarella.

2. Evenly scatter over the spinach and tightly roll up each tortilla. Cut in half to serve.

I can help spread the pesto and top the tortillas with chicken, mozzarella and spinach

Mexican wraps

Makes
8 halves

Prep time
10 minutes

Ingredients

400g can black beans, drained

5 tablespoons roughly chopped fresh coriander

3 spring onions or ½ small red onion, roughly chopped

Juice of 1 lime

4 wholewheat or seeded tortillas

1 avocado, sliced

2 tomatoes, sliced

75g Cheddar cheese, grated

2 tablespoons soured cream

Method

1. Put the black beans in a food processor with the coriander, chopped onion and lime juice. Whiz to form a smooth paste and season to taste.

2. Place the tortillas on the kitchen surface and spread one-quarter of the bean paste over each one. Top each with one-quarter of the sliced avocado, sliced tomato and grated cheese.

3. Drizzle ½ tablespoon soured cream over each tortilla. Tightly roll the tortillas and cut in half to serve.

I can help spread the bean paste over the wraps and layer the avocado, tomato and cheese

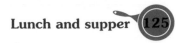

Hummus and carrot wraps

Makes

8 halves

Prep time

5 minutes

Ingredients

4 wholewheat or seeded tortillas

150g Hummus (p.137 or use store-bought)

2 carrots, grated

12 cucumber slices or a handful of fresh spinach leaves

Method

1. Place the tortillas on the kitchen surface and spread hummus over each one. Top each with the grated carrot and slices of cucumber or spinach.

2. Tightly roll the tortillas and cut in half to serve.

I can help grate the carrot and spread hummus on the tortillas

Fish fingers

Makes
12 fingers

Prep time
15 minutes

Cook time
12–15 minutes

Ingredients

500g sustainable white fish fillets, eg cod, skinned

2 tablespoons plain flour

1 medium free-range egg, beaten

100g panko or dried natural breadcrumbs

1 tablespoon finely chopped fresh flat-leaf parsley

2 tablespoons grated Parmesan cheese

1 tablespoon melted butter

½ teaspoon salt (optional)

Method

1. Preheat the oven to 200°C/gas mark 6. Line a baking tray with baking parchment.

2. Cut the fish into 12 2 x 8cm long strips and set aside. Place the flour on a plate and the beaten egg into a shallow bowl. Mix together the breadcrumbs, parsley, Parmesan, butter and salt in another bowl.

3. Take the strips and dip first into the flour and shake off the excess, then dip into the egg letting any excess drip off. Then finally gently roll in the breadcrumbs. Place the crumbed fingers onto the lined tray. Bake for 12–15 minutes or until lightly golden and cooked through.

4. Serve with Sweet potato chips (p.100), peas and Tartare sauce (p.71).

I can help dip the fish in the flour, egg and breadcrumbs

Tuna melt

This is a fancier version of a cheese toasty with a bit more protein when energy levels need a boost.

Makes
3 sandwiches

Prep time
10 minutes

Cook time
8–10 minutes

Ingredients

200g can tuna in spring water, drained

2 tablespoons mayonnaise

6 slices of sourdough or wholemeal bread

1 large tomato, sliced

60g cheese, eg Cheddar or mozzarella or a mixture, grated

Method

1. Preheat oven to 200°C/gas mark 6.

2. Mix the tuna and mayonnaise together in a bowl. Lightly toast the bread then top 3 slices with the tuna mix, a slice or two of tomato followed by the grated cheese.

3. Top the sandwiches with the remaining lightly toasted slices of bread. Place on a non-stick baking tray and bake for 8–10 minutes or until the cheese has melted.

I can help mix the tuna and mayonnaise and spread on the toast

Savoury snacks

In this section we have made a special effort to focus on savoury snacks instead of sweet snacks (which seem to be in abundance). The recipes we've pulled together here are great for after-school or on-the-go picnics.

Healthier sausage rolls

These are made using either turkey or chicken mince, and in our experience, children love them. You can easily substitute the Sausage patties recipe on p.39 if you want a more traditional version.

Makes

48 rolls

Prep time

15 minutes
plus chilling

Cook time

25 minutes

Ingredients

500g minced turkey or pork

1 teaspoon dried sage

1 teaspoon dried thyme

½ teaspoon grated nutmeg

2 medium free-range eggs, lightly beaten

1 medium courgette, finely grated and excess moisture squeezed out

1 small carrot, finely grated

Flour, for dusting

2cm puff pastry sheets, halved lengthways

1 tablespoon milk

Sesame seeds and poppy seeds, for sprinkling

Salt and freshly ground black pepper (optional)

Method

1. In a large bowl, mix together the minced turkey or pork, sage, thyme, nutmeg, one egg, courgette and carrot. Season, cover and place in the fridge for 30 minutes.

2. Preheat the oven to 200°C/gas mark 6. Line a baking sheet with baking parchment.

3. Place the pasty sheets on a floured work surface.

4. Roll the meat mixture into four long sausage-shaped rolls the same length as the pastry and then lay each one along the centre of each piece of pastry.

5. Mix the remaining egg and milk together in a small bowl and brush the pastry edges with the mixture. Fold the long side of the pastry over the filling and press the pastry with your fingers or the edges of a fork to seal.

6. Cut the rolls into 2cm pieces and place on the baking sheet, leaving a good gap between each one. Brush each one with more of the egg and milk wash and sprinkle with poppy and sesame seeds. Bake for 20–25 minutes or until golden and cooked through. Transfer to a wired rack to cool.

Tip: *To freeze sausage rolls, place them, uncooked in the freezer on a baking sheet. Once frozen transfer them to freezer bags or an airtight container. Cook from frozen, as above, for 30–35 minutes, or until they are puffed, golden and piping hot.*

I can help combine the meat mixture in a bowl with my hands and brush the pastry edges. I always remember to wash my hands well after touching raw meat.

Courgette and feta muffins

Makes

12 muffins

Prep time

10 minutes

Cook time

25 minutes

Ingredients

200g white spelt flour

1 teaspoon bicarbonate of soda

½ teaspoon smoked paprika

1 tablespoon ground flaxseed

Pinch of sea salt

100ml olive oil

150ml Greek yoghurt

2 large free-range eggs

175g courgette, coarsely grated and excess moisture squeezed out

100g feta cheese, crumbled

1 teaspoon dried oregano

Butter for greasing

Method

1. Preheat the oven to 190°C/gas mark 5. Grease a 12-hole muffin tin or line with paper muffin cases.

2. Sift the flour and bicarbonate of soda into a large bowl. Add the paprika, flaxseed and salt.

3. In a separate bowl, whisk together the olive oil, yoghurt and eggs. Pour this into the flour mixture. Gently stir in the courgette, feta cheese and herbs; do not over-mix or the muffins will be tough.

4. Use an ice cream scoop to divide the mixture evenly between the muffin cases. Bake for 25 minutes or until cooked and golden. Remove and leave in the tin for 10 minutes. Transfer to a wire rack and cool.

I can help to crumble the feta cheese, grate and squeeze out any of the excess moisture from the courgette before adding to the bowl

Homemade chorizo

These chorizo meatballs are great for a picnic or play date.
We make two versions – I add ¼ teaspoon of cayenne pepper
for the grown-ups.

Serves

a family of 4 or
6 children

Prep time

10 minutes plus
chilling

Cook time

8–10 minutes

*I can help
combine the
mixture in the
bowl with my hands
and shape into
meatballs. I always
remember to wash
my hands well
after touching
raw meat*

Ingredients

500g minced pork

2 garlic cloves, peeled and grated

1 tablespoon smoked paprika

1 teaspoon salt (optional)

½ teaspoon fennel seeds

2 tablespoons oil

Method

1. Place all the ingredients, except the oil, in a large bowl and mix well using your hands. Shape the mixture into evenly-sized meatballs. Place on a tray and chill in the fridge for 10 minutes.

2. Heat a large non-stick frying pan over a medium heat. Add the oil and when hot but not smoking, add the meatballs. Cook for 8–10 until cooked through, turning every couple of minutes.

Hummus

Hummus is a quick and easy dip that children love. Serve with homemade pitta chips (p.142) or cut-up vegetables. The flavours develop overnight in the fridge if you can make it a day in advance.

Makes
345g

Prep time
5 minutes

Ingredients

400g can chickpeas, drained and rinsed

2 tablespoons lemon juice

1–2 small garlic cloves, peeled

2 tablespoons tahini

6 tablespoons olive oil

¼ teaspoon salt (optional)

¼ teaspoon cumin (optional)

Method

1. Put the chickpeas, lemon juice, garlic and tahini into a food processor and whiz. Add the olive oil, salt and cumin and whiz again. For a smoother mixture, add 2–3 tablespoons water as needed and whiz again.

2. Cover and chill for 2–3 days.

Beetroot hummus

Makes
400g

Prep time
5–10 minutes

Ingredients

400g can chickpeas, drained and rinsed

125g cooked beetroot

2 tablespoons lemon juice

1 small garlic clove, peeled

2 tablespoons tahini

6 tablespoons olive oil

¼ teaspoon salt (optional)

Method

1. Put the chickpeas, beetroot, lemon juice, garlic and tahini into a food processor and whiz. Add the olive oil and salt and whiz again. For a smoother mixture, add 2–3 tablespoons water and whiz again.

2. Cover and chill for up to 2 days.

Tip: *This is great with a bit of crumbled feta.*

Green pea hummus

Makes
550g

Prep time
10–15 minutes

Ingredients

400g canned chickpeas, drained and rinsed

400g cooked frozen peas

2 tablespoons lemon juice

1–2 small garlic cloves, peeled

2 tablespoons tahini

6 tablespoons olive oil

¼ teaspoon salt (optional)

1 tablespoon finely chopped fresh mint

Method

1. Put the chickpeas, cooked frozen peas, lemon juice, garlic and tahini into a food processor and whiz. Add the olive oil, salt and fresh mint and whiz again. For a smoother mixture, add 2 tablespoons water and whiz again.

2. Cover and chill for up to 2 days.

Pitta chips

Serves

a family of 4 or
6 children

Prep time

5 minutes

Cook time

10–12 minutes

Ingredients

2 round wholemeal pitta breads

2 tablespoons olive oil

Optional toppings

2 teaspoons sesame seeds

2 teaspoons grated Parmesan cheese

Method

1. Preheat the oven to 180°C/gas mark 4. Line two large baking sheets with baking parchment.

2. Split each of the pitta breads in half and cut into 6 wedges. Brush with the olive oil and sprinkle with the sesame seeds or Parmesan if using.

3. Arrange the pitta wedges on the prepared baking sheets and bake for 10–12 minutes. Remove and serve hot, or allow to cool and store in an airtight container for up to 2 days.

I can help brush the pitta bread with a little olive oil and sprinkle on the sesame seeds or Parmesan cheese

Smoked salmon finger sandwiches

Serves

2–4 children

Prep time

5–10 minutes

Ingredients

1 packet soft cream cheese

8 slices wholegrain bread

100g smoked salmon

16 thin slices cucumber

Juice of ¼ lemon

Method

1. Spread a thin layer of cream cheese on 4 slices of the bread. Then top each slice with a quarter of the smoked salmon and 4 cucumber slices.

2. Squeeze on the lemon juice then top with remaining bread and cut the crusts off. Cut the sandwiches into fingers or triangles and serve straight away.

I can help spread the cream cheese and assemble the sandwiches

Cheese straws

Makes
about 12 long or
24 short straws

Prep time
15 minutes

Cook time
8–10 minutes

Ingredients

100g Cheddar cheese, grated

50g Parmesan cheese, grated

100g plain flour, plus extra for dusting

Small pinch of cayenne pepper

¼ teaspoon black pepper (optional)

100g chilled butter, cut into ¼cm cubes

1 medium free-range egg yolk

Method

1. Preheat the oven to 220°C/gas mark 7. Line a baking sheet with baking parchment.

2. Place the grated cheeses into a large mixing bowl. Sift in the flour and add the cayenne pepper and black pepper. Add the butter cubes and rub together with your fingertips. When the mixture resembles coarse breadcrumbs, pour in the egg yolk and stir with a knife. Bring the dough together to form a ball and tip onto a lightly floured surface.

3. Shape the dough into a rectangle and then roll until 5mm thick. Trim the edges so you have neat sides. Cut the rectangle into 2cm strips. Place the strips carefully onto the baking sheet, leaving a little room between each one as they will spread during cooking.

4. Bake for 8–10 minutes or until the cheese straws are cooked and golden. Remove from the oven and leave them to cool on the tray for 5 minutes. Then transfer to a wire rack and leave to cool completely.

5. Store in an airtight container for 2–3 days.

I can help rub the mixture with my fingertips until it's a crumbly texture; and also help roll out the dough and cut it into strips

Smoked mackerel pâté

Makes

400g

Prep time

15 minutes
plus flaking fish
off bones and
chilling time

Ingredients

250g soft cream cheese

175g smoked mackerel, skinned, boned and flaked

1–2 teaspoons horseradish sauce

2 teaspoons lemon juice

Pitta chips (p.142), to serve

Method

1. Mix all the ingredients together, transfer to a small serving dish and chill for
an hour. Serve with Pitta chips for dipping.

2. Cover leftovers and keep in the fridge for up to 3 days

*I can help
mix all the
ingredients
together*

Puddings and treats

This next section is a collection of our favourite puddings and treats to make with little helpers. It's especially nice to prepare your own desserts because you know exactly what ingredients go into them. We have made an effort to reduce sugar levels in many of these recipes and they were still loved by all of our tiny tasters.

Eton mess

Serves

a family of 4 with leftovers or 8 children

Prep time

15 minutes

Ingredients

480ml double cream

½ teaspoon vanilla extract

250g strawberries, hulled and sliced

175g raspberries

1 tablespoon Demerara sugar

1 teaspoon balsamic vinegar

125g meringues, crushed

Method

1. Whip the cream in a bowl until it is firm, then stir in the vanilla extract.

2. In a separate bowl, combine half the fruit, the sugar and balsamic vinegar, and mash with a fork until the consistency resembles stewed fruit.

3. In a serving dish, roughly mix together the cream, mashed fruit and crumbled meringues. Scatter the remaining fruit on top and serve at once.

Tip: This can also be made without the Demerara sugar as the meringue contributes a lot of sweetness.

I can help crush the meringues and mash the fruit

Peanut butter squares

Children can help press the base down in the pan (and bash the biscuits if you don't use a food processor).

Makes

16 squares

Prep time

15 minutes plus overnight chilling

Cook time

5 minutes

Ingredients

200g dark chocolate, broken into pieces

150g butter

250g digestive biscuits (or substitute ginger biscuits)

100g dark brown sugar

300g crunchy peanut butter

1 teaspoon vanilla extract

Method

1. Line a 20cm square cake tin with a square of parchment paper large enough to come up higher than the sides of the tin.

2. Place the chocolate in a heatproof bowl over a pan of simmering water, stir occasionally and once melted set aside. Melt the butter in a medium pan over a very low heat, remove from the heat and set aside.

3. Blitz the biscuits into fine crumbs either in a food processor, or place them in a plastic bag and bash them with a rolling pin. Stir the biscuits into the butter with the brown sugar, peanut butter and vanilla extract. Mix until everything is well combined.

4. Pour the mixture into the lined cake tin and then smooth out with the back of a spoon. Pour the chocolate on top of the mixture and spread to cover evenly. Chill in the fridge overnight.

5. Remove from the tin, using the paper to help pull it out. Cut into 16 squares and keep in the fridge for 2–3 days.

I can help bash the biscuits, mix the ingredients and press the mixture down in the pan

Blackberry and apple parcels

These are fun to make on a play date with a friend
as you can divide up the parcels to fill and assemble.

Makes

6 rectangular
parcels

Prep time
20 minutes

Cook time
25 minutes

Ingredients

300g apples, chopped

75g soft brown sugar

200g blackberries

½ teaspoon vanilla extract

2 packs 320g ready-rolled puff pastry

1 medium free-range egg, beaten

1 teaspoon Demerara sugar (optional)

Method

1. Preheat the oven to 180°C/gas mark 4.

2. Place the apples in a medium pan with the soft brown sugar. Cook over a medium heat, for 5 minutes, or until the apples are soft. Set aside to cool for 5 minutes. Stir in the blackberries and vanilla extract.

3. Cut the pastry into 6 x 10cm rectangles. Using a slotted spoon, divide the fruit mixture, equally, between half the pastry rectangles, leaving a 1–2cm border.

4. Brush the borders of the topped pastry rectangles with the beaten egg. Place the remaining pastry pieces over the top, pressing the edges down with a fork to seal in the filling. Make 2 slits in the top of each pie to let the steam escape.

5. Brush the parcels with the beaten egg and sprinkle with the Demerara sugar, if using. Bake for 25 minutes or until golden and cooked through. Leave to cool for 5 minutes and transfer to a wire rack.

I can help spoon the fruit onto the parcels and brush the border of the pastry with the beaten egg

Banana bread

Makes
1 x 900g loaf

Prep time
10 minutes

Cook time
45–50 minutes

Ingredients

Butter, for greasing

60ml coconut oil

125ml maple syrup

1 teaspoon vanilla extract

2 medium free-range eggs, beaten

200g white spelt flour

1 tablespoon ground flaxseed

1 teaspoon baking powder

½ teaspoon bicarbonate of soda

320g ripe bananas, mashed (about 3 bananas)

2 tablespoons natural or Greek yoghurt

Drizzle of honey, to serve (optional)

Method

1. Preheat the oven to 180°C/gas mark 4. Lightly grease a 900g loaf tin.

2. Mix the oil and syrup together in a bowl and then stir in the vanilla extract and beaten eggs. Gently fold in the flour, flaxseed, baking powder and bicarbonate of soda. Then stir in the banana and yoghurt.

3. Spoon the cake batter into the tin and smooth the top with a palette knife. Bake the cake for 45–50 minutes or until a skewer inserted into the centre of the cake comes out clean.

4. Remove the cake from the oven and leave to cool for 5 minutes. Transfer to a cooling rack, drizzle the top with honey (if using) and allow to cool completely.

Tip: This is also delicious with pecan nuts. Add 50g of roughly chopped pecans to the batter with the banana and yoghurt.

I can help mash the bananas and mix the ingredients together in the bowl

Chocolate and hazelnut spread

Great on toast, oat biscuits or warm Banana bread (p.156).

Makes

1 large jar

Prep time

15 minutes

Ingredients

270g whole hazelnuts, unpeeled and roasted

3 tablespoons cocoa powder

200g honey

125ml water

Method

1. Whiz hazelnuts and cocoa powder in a food processor for about 10 minutes until the mixture is paste-like.

2. Slowly add honey and blend to combine.

3. Pour in half of the water and check consistency. Add more water as needed to get the consistency you want.

4. Pour into a jar, seal and store in the fridge for up to 2 weeks.

I can help measure out the ingredients and add them to the food processor

Vanilla custard

The perfect addition to Fruit crumble (p.161) or Baked apples (p.162).

Makes

1 litre

Prep time

5 minutes

Cook time

10 minutes

Ingredients

1 litre full-fat milk

6 medium free-range egg yolks

100g caster sugar

Pinch of salt (optional)

2 tablespoons cornflour mixed with a small amount of cold water

1 teaspoon vanilla extract

Method

1. Prepare a saucepan of simmering water. You will also need a heatproof bowl that fits on the top of the pan.

2. Place the milk in a small pan and bring it almost to the boil.

3. Lightly beat the egg yolks, sugar and salt in the heatproof bowl (off the heat). Gradually stir in the hot milk. Sit the bowl on top of the pan of simmering water and stir in the cornflour. Continue to stir until it thickens enough to coat the spoon.

4. Take the custard off the heat and add the vanilla extract.

Tips: If the custard starts to go lumpy, place the bowl in cold water and beat until smooth.

I can help crack the eggs and separate the yolks

Fruit crumble

This recipe can be made in advance and kept in the fridge for up to 24 hours. You can put it in the oven as you sit down to supper and you'll have a lovely warm crumble in time for dessert. Top with the custard on p.159 or vanilla ice cream.

Serves
a family of 4 with leftovers or 8 children

Prep time
10 minutes

Cook time
35–40 minutes

Ingredients

Butter, for greasing

For the filling

600g mixed fruit (eg eating apples, berries, plums, pears), prepared and cut into bite-size pieces

1 tablespoon lemon juice

2 tablespoons soft brown sugar

1 teaspoon vanilla extract

For the topping

50g soft brown sugar

80g rolled porridge oats

100g plain flour

1 tablespoon flaxseed

Pinch of ground cinnamon

Pinch of salt (optional)

90g unsalted butter, at room temperature, cut into pieces

I can help combine the butter in the flour with my fingertips and sprinkle the topping over the fruit

Method

1. Preheat the oven to 200°C/gas mark 6. Lightly grease a 23cm square baking dish.

2. Place the fruit, lemon juice, brown sugar and vanilla extract in the baking dish and toss together.

3. For the topping, combine all the dry ingredients in a medium bowl and rub in the butter, using your fingertips, until the consistency resembles coarse breadcrumbs. Sprinkle the topping over the fruit.

4. Place the dish on a baking tray and bake for 35 minutes or until the fruit is bubbling and the topping is browned.

Baked apples

Even your littlest one can help fill the apples with dried fruit.

Makes
6 apples

Prep time
15 minutes

Cook time
25 minutes

Ingredients

6 eating apples

Juice of 1 lemon

50g sultanas

50g dried cranberries

1 tablespoon light muscovado sugar

½ teaspoon ground cinnamon

15g butter

1 teaspoon Demerara sugar

Method

1. Preheat the oven to 200°C/gas mark 6.

2. Core the apples, using an apple corer or a sharp knife. Using a small knife, score a horizontal line around the middle of each apple. Squeeze lemon juice over the prepared apples to stop them browning. Place the apples in a medium baking dish.

3. In a small bowl mix together the sultanas, dried cranberries, muscovado sugar and cinnamon. Push a little of the mixture into each apple. Dot the butter over the top of each apple and then sprinkle with Demerara sugar.

4. Bake the apples for 25 minutes or until cooked through.

I can help fill the apples with dried fruit and sprinkle on the sugar

Fruit kebabs

These kebabs work with any fruit you have on hand and are fun for picnics. Older children can carefully help put the fruit on the skewers.

Makes
8 kebabs

Prep time
15 minutes

Ingredients

Juice of ½ lemon

2 bananas, cut into 2.5cm slices

5 large strawberries, halved

2 kiwi fruit, thickly sliced, each slice cut into 6 equal chunks

1 melon, de-seeded and cut into large chunks

Method

Drizzle the lemon juice over the banana slices to stop them going brown. Arrange alternate pieces of fruit on 8 wooden skewers and serve immediately.

I can help carefully put the fruit on the wooden skewers

Oaty chocolate chip cookies

Children of all ages can help form the batter into balls and then flatten gently with a fork.

Makes

36 small cookies

Prep time

15 minutes

Cook time

10–12 minutes

Ingredients

115g butter

100g soft light brown sugar

1 medium free-range egg

1 teaspoon vanilla extract

140g plain flour

125g jumbo rolled oats

½ teaspoon baking powder

½ teaspoon bicarbonate of soda

100g chocolate chips

Method

1. Preheat the oven to 190°C/gas mark 5. Line two baking sheets with baking parchment.

2. In a large bowl, cream together the butter and sugar. Add the egg and beat until well combined. Stir in the vanilla extract.

3. In another large bowl combine the flour, oats, baking powder and bicarbonate of soda. Add to the egg mixture and beat together. Stir in the chocolate chips.

4. Roll the mixture into 2cm balls and space them well apart on the baking sheets, press each gently with a fork to flatten slightly.

5. Bake in the oven for 10–12 minutes or until golden. Leave to cool on the sheet for 2 minutes and then transfer to a cooling rack to cool completely.

6. The cookies can be stored in an airtight container for 2–3 days or up to 1 week in the fridge.

Tip: You can freeze the flattened cookies before baking. Cook from frozen for 12–14 minutes at 190°C

I can help roll the batter into balls and press down with a fork

Homemade Jammy dodgers

For traditional biscuits, use a larger round cookie cutter approximately 5cm across. But any shapes will work. You'll also need a smaller circle or shape to cut holes out of the top biscuits.

Makes

24 biscuits

Prep time

20 minutes
plus chilling

Cook time

10–12 minutes

Ingredients

225g unsalted butter, softened

80g brown sugar

200g plain flour

100g ground almonds

100g raspberry jam

1 medium free-range egg, beaten

Method

1. Preheat the oven to 190°C/gas mark 5. Line 2 baking trays with baking parchment.

2. Place the butter, sugar, flour and almonds in a large bowl or a food processor. Either rub the mixture together with your fingertips, until a dough is formed or whiz in the food processor until the mixture just comes together. Roll the dough between 2 sheets of cling film to about 1cm thickness. Chill in the fridge for 1 hour.

3. Remove the top piece of clingfilm and using a 5cm round cutter, stamp out 48 biscuits. (If the dough gets sticky chill it for 10 minutes.)

4. Place half of the dough rounds onto a lined baking tray. With a 2cm round cutter or a small shaped cutter stamp out the centres from the remaining dough rounds.

5. Brush the circle edges with a little whisked egg and put a teaspoon of raspberry jam in the centre of each biscuit (don't use too much or it will spill out during cooking). Spread the jam out a little using the back of a spoon, then top with the dough rings. Bake the biscuits for 10–12 minutes or until golden and cooked. Leave to cool for 5 minutes and transfer to a wire rack.

6. Keep in an airtight container for 3–5 days.

I can use cookie cutters to cut the biscuits, and spread on the raspberry jam

Peanut butter 'ice cream'

Serves
4

Prep time
5 minutes plus
freezing

Ingredients

100g Greek yoghurt

100ml full-fat milk

6 tablespoons smooth peanut butter

3 tablespoons honey

1 teaspoon ground cinnamon

2 teaspoons vanilla extract

1 ripe banana

20g plain chocolate, grated (optional)

Method

1. Whisk the yoghurt, milk, peanut butter, honey, cinnamon and vanilla extract together in a medium bowl. Mash the banana well and stir into the mixture. Divide the mixture between 4 ramekins and cover each ramekin with cling film.

2. Freeze the ramekins for a few hours. Remove from the freezer and sprinkle the chocolate (if using) over each ramekin and serve.

I can help mix the ingredients together and mash the banana

Fruit sorbet

Serves
a family of 4 or
6 children

Prep time
10 minutes

Ingredients

2 bananas, sliced

300g frozen mixed berries

100g plain yoghurt

1 teaspoon honey

Method

1. Put all the ingredients into a blender and whiz until smooth. Use an ice cream scoop to serve immediately.

I can help measure out the ingredients and add them to the blender

Flourless mini chocolate cakes

These chocolate cakes are gluten free and very chocolaty.
They are a fun treat in small portions.

Makes

32 little cakes

Prep time

30 minutes

Cook time

7–10 minutes

Ingredients

100g unsalted butter, plus extra for greasing

300g plain chocolate, broken into pieces

4 medium free-range eggs

3 tablespoons brown sugar

Pinch of salt (optional)

3 tablespoons arrowroot

Method

1. Preheat the oven to 200°C/gas mark 6. Grease a mini muffin tray.

2. Place the butter and chocolate in a large heatproof bowl over a pan of simmering water, stir occasionally and once melted set aside to cool.

3. Meanwhile, crack the eggs and add sugar in a separate large bowl, and with a hand-held electric whisk, beat on a high speed for 4–5 minutes or until pale and creamy.

4. Stir the salt and arrowroot into the melted chocolate until combined. Pour half of the egg mixture into the chocolate, stirring gently. Stir in the remaining half until well combined.

5. Half fill the muffin tins with the chocolate mixture and bake for 7–10 minutes.

I can help crack the eggs and spoon the mixture into the muffin tins

Raspberry sponge

Children love to mix the ingredients and help crush the raspberries.
We didn't add cream to this version, but it is a great optional addition.

Makes

1 x 18cm cake

Prep time
10 minutes

Cook time
20–25 minutes

Ingredients

4 tablespoons rapeseed oil plus extra for greasing

150g self-raising flour

2 teaspoons baking powder

100g golden caster sugar

50g ground almonds

2 medium free-range eggs

150g natural yoghurt

2 teaspoons vanilla extract

3 tablespoons milk

150g fresh raspberries

2 teaspoons honey

2 teaspoons icing sugar, sifted

Method

1. Preheat the oven to 180°C/gas mark 4. Grease and line 2 x 18cm loose-bottomed sandwich tins with baking parchment.

2. In a large bowl mix together the flour, baking powder, caster sugar and ground almonds. Mix the eggs in a large jug and stir in the yoghurt, vanilla, oil and milk. Pour the egg mixture into the flour mixture, and stir until the ingredients just come together Pour the mixture into the prepared tins.

3. Bake in the oven for 20–25 minutes or until a skewer inserted into the centre comes out clean.

4. Meanwhile, lightly crush the raspberries using a fork. Stir in the honey and set aside.

5. Remove the cakes from the oven. Allow to cool in the tins for 5 minutes. Turn out onto a wire rack and allow to cool completely.

6. When completely cool, spread the raspberry mixture over the top of one of the sponges. Top with the other sponge and dust with icing sugar.

I can help crush the raspberries and sprinkle on the icing sugar

Grandma's lemon cake

This was a popular recipe from our first cookbook. We have since halved the sugar and it's still sweet and loved by children. They can help grate and squeeze the lemons.

Makes
1 x 900g loaf

Prep time
15 minutes

Cook time
45–50 minutes

Ingredients

175g unsalted butter at room temperature, plus extra for greasing

100g caster sugar

3 medium free-range eggs

Zest and juice of 1 lemon

200g self-raising flour

30g ground almonds

1 tablespoon boiled water

For the topping

6 tablespoons icing sugar, sifted

2 tablespoons lemon juice

Method

1. Preheat the oven to 180°C/gas mark 4. Lightly grease a 900g loaf tin.

2. Place the butter and sugar in a large bowl and beat together, using a hand-held electric whisk, until light and fluffy. Beat in the eggs, one at a time, and then add the lemon zest and juice. Fold in the flour and ground almonds. Stir in the boiled water to bring the mixture to a smooth consistency.

3. Pour the cake mixture into the loaf tin and bake for 45–50 minutes until well risen and golden.

4. To make the topping, mix the icing sugar and lemon juice together in a small bowl. The consistency will be quite runny. Pour over the cake while it is still in the tin, immediately after it comes out of the oven. Leave the cake in the tin to cool and then transfer to a wire rack to cool completely.

I can help zest and juice the lemon and add ingredients to the bowl

Gluten-free carrot cake

This cake is surprisingly delicious considering it is gluten free. Children can help juice the orange, which is what makes it so moist. Serve on its own or with Cream cheese frosting (below).

Makes
1 x 20cm cake

Prep time
15 minutes

Cook time
45–50 minutes

Ingredients

150g unsalted butter, softened

100g caster sugar

300g carrots, coarsely grated

2 medium free-range eggs, lightly beaten

200g gluten-free self-raising flour

1 teaspoon ground cinnamon

½ teaspoon ground nutmeg

1 teaspoon gluten-free baking powder

Juice of 1 orange

50g walnuts, roughly chopped

Cream cheese frosting, to serve (optional)

Method

1. Preheat the oven to 180°C/gas mark 4. Grease and line a 20cm round, loose-based cake tin with baking parchment.

2. In a large bowl beat together the butter and sugar until pale and creamy. Stir in the grated carrot. Gradually stir in the eggs. Then gently fold in the flour, cinnamon, nutmeg, baking powder and orange juice. Stir in the walnuts and tip the mixture into the cake tin.

3. Bake for 45–50 minutes or until a skewer inserted into the centre of the cake comes out clean.

4. Allow the cake to cool in the tin for 15 minutes and then turn out onto a cooling rack to cool completely. This keeps in the fridge for a few days.

I can help grate the carrots and juice the orange

Cream cheese frosting

Ingredients

100g cream cheese

100g mascarpone cheese

75g icing sugar, sifted

Method

In a large bowl, beat together the cream cheese, mascarpone and icing sugar.

Fruit coulis

Serves

a family of 4 or
6 children

Prep time

5 minutes

Ingredients

300g raspberries or a mixture of raspberries and strawberries

1 tablespoon honey

Juice of ½ lemon

Method

1. Place the fruit in a blender and whiz into a smooth purée. Add the honey and lemon juice. For a thinner consistency, add a little water. Perfect with ice cream.

Chocolate coconut sauce

Serves

6–8

Prep time

5 minutes

I can measure the ingredients and stir them together

Ingredients

8 tablespoons coconut oil, melted

4 tablespoons honey

6 tablespoons cocoa powder, sifted

2 teaspoons vanilla extract

Method

1. Mix all the ingredients together in a jug until well combined and then pour into a lidded plastic container. Store in the fridge for up to a week.

2. When ready to serve, if the mixture is too thick, stir in a little hot water over a low heat in a saucepan.

3. Serve with vanilla ice cream.

Orange and almond cake

Makes

1 x 20cm cake

Prep time

1 hour

Cook time

40–45 minutes

Ingredients

For the cake

110g butter, softened plus extra for greasing

2 large oranges

110g plain flour

1 teaspoon baking power

¼ teaspoon salt (optional)

110g ground almonds

100g caster sugar

1 teaspoon vanilla extract

3 medium free-range eggs

For the honey-glazed oranges

1 orange

100g honey

125ml water

Method

1. Preheat the oven to 180°C/gas mark 4. Grease and line an 20cm round cake tin with baking parchment.

2. Place one of the oranges, whole and unpeeled, in a saucepan and cover with boiling water. Simmer for 45 minutes or until it is soft. Remove the cooked orange and set aside to cool. Meanwhile zest the second orange (the orange itself is not needed in this recipe).

3. Place the flour, baking powder, salt, ground almonds and orange zest in a large bowl and mix to combine.

4. In a separate large bowl, cream the butter, sugar and vanilla extract together, using a hand-held electric whisk, until light and fluffy. Beat in the eggs.

5. Once the cooked orange has cooled, cut it into several pieces, and whiz the whole thing in a food processor to form a smooth purée. Add the orange purée to the creamed mixture. Then stir in the dry ingredients and fold together until just combined.

6. Pour the mixture into the prepared cake tin and bake for 40–45 minutes or until golden on top and a skewer inserted into the centre comes out clean.

7. While the cake is baking, prepare the glaze topping. Cut the orange into 7–8 thin slices. Place the slices in a pan and add the honey and water. Bring to the boil, then simmer for 15 minutes until the liquid starts to become syrupy.

8. Remove the cake from the oven and use a wooden skewer to pierce several holes in the top. While the cake is still warm, spoon the honey syrup over it and arrange the orange slices on top. Leave the cake to cool in the tin, on a wire rack. Once completely cool, remove from the tin, transfer to a plate.

I can help zest the orange and mix ingredients together

Eating the rainbow

Most of us know about the importance of eating at least five portions of fruit and veg every day. But did you know that it's also important to eat as many different colours of fruit and veg as possible? That's because they contain some amazingly powerful nutrients called phytonutrients which are only naturally available in plants. By eating as many colours as possible, we're getting the broadest range of benefits we can.

How many colours of the rainbow do you eat each day?

Red and Pink

eg tomatoes, red peppers, strawberries, raspberries, watermelon, pomegranate, cranberries

Berry healthy – children need folic acid for good brain development and berries contain the highest levels of folic acid of any fruit. Berries are also packed with Vitamin C and antioxidants which give little immune systems a boost and help fight off infection.

Yellow and Orange

eg carrots, sweet potato, butternut squash, pumpkin, orange peppers, mangoes, cantaloupe melon, apricots

Do carrots really help you see in the dark? Orange fruit and veg contain carotenoids which are thought to support healthy eyes and skin.

Green

eg broccoli, cabbage, brussels sprouts, spinach, peas, green beans, asparagus, avocado, kiwi fruit

Eat your greens – dark green veg may help protect against serious illnesses like cancer and heart disease. Leafy greens are also a source of vitamin K which helps with blood clotting – good for healing little grazed knees.

Purple and Blue

eg beetroot, aubergine, red onions, blueberries, blackberries, prunes, plums, red grapes, cherries

Purple and blue fruit and veg can improve brain power and encourage healthy memory – good for little learners.

White

eg cauliflower, mushrooms, chick peas, garlic, almonds, oats

Even onions and garlic are little nutrient powerhouses, containing phytonutrients such as quercetin and allicin, known to kill harmful bacteria and support healthy circulation.

Index

Acknowledgements

Thank you to the following recipe contributors, developers, testers and helpers:

Clare Woodman, Estee Mathias, Emma Brocksom, Katie Giovanni, Caitlin Reynolds, Julia Azzarello, Dean Brown, Monty Brown, Ridley Brown, Tabitha Tisdall, Eva Tisdall, Indie Hulton, Dale Graves, Ann Brown, Elizabeth Beebe, Lisa Onia and Jane Hunter.

And also to the marketing, design and editorial team:

Charlotte Tisdall, Josi Gilgallon, Nancy Evans, Adam Strange, Sian Rance and Rhiannon Smith.

Little chef stars and other sticker fun

Each time your little helper tries a new skill, help them choose a sticker for their skills chart (p.10) as an award for their achievement. Before you know it, they'll earn their little chef's apron.

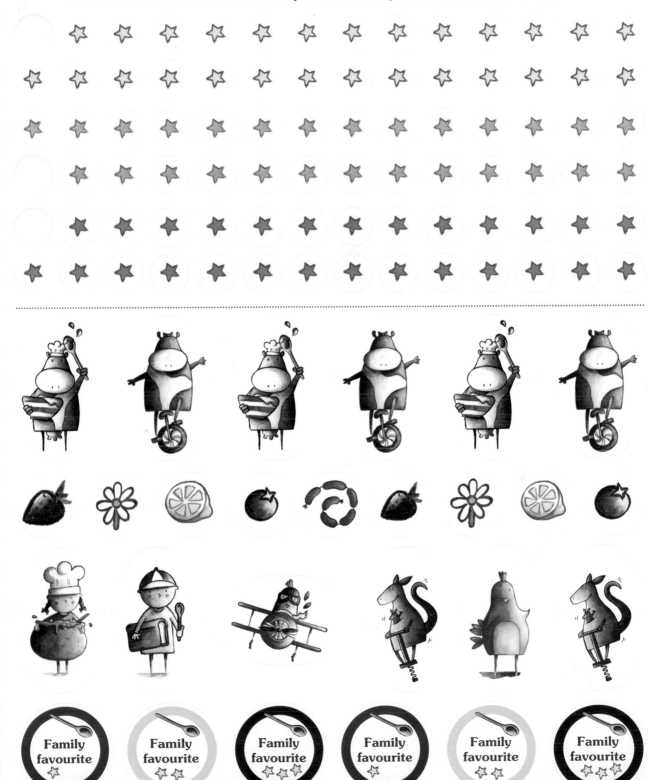